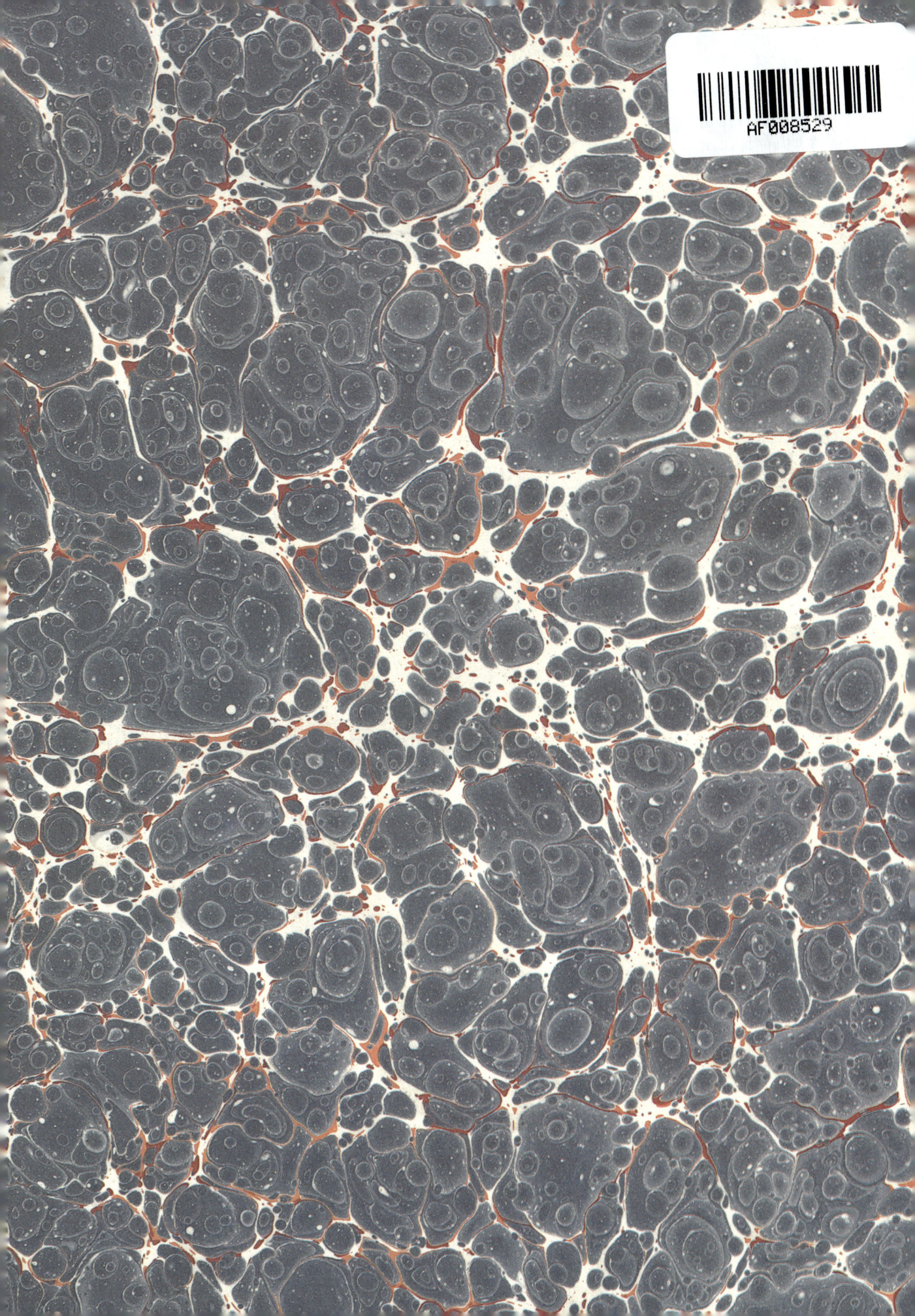

Nauroth/Held • Messerschmitt Bf 110

HOLGER NAUROTH/WERNER HELD

Messerschmitt Bf 110

Over all fronts 1939-1945

SCHIFFER MILITARY HISTORY
West Chester, PA

Photos: Schob 179, Nauroth 149, Jabs 40, Nacke 40, Federal Archives 38, Falck 22, Ziegenhagen 17, Diener 11, Dombrowsky 6, Jäger 4, Freitag 3, United States Air Force 1.

Sources: Bekker, *Angriffshöhe 4000*; Girbig, *Jagdgeschwader 5 "Eismeerjäger"*; Obermeier, *Ritterkreuzträger*; Kens-Novarra, *Die deutschen Flugzeuge von 35-45*; Karl Ries, *Markierungen und Tarnanstriche der Luftwaffe I-IV*; Karl Ries, *Dora Kurfürst und rote Dreizehn I-IV*; Ries-Ahnert, *Die deutsche Luftwaffe von 39-45*; Feuchter, *Luftkrieg*; Tippelskirch, *Geschichte des II. Weltkrieges*.

Editors Note: The term *Zerstörer* (destroyer) refers to a twin-engine, long range fighter/bomber of the Bf 110 type.

Translated from the German by Dr. Edward Force,
Central Connecticut State University.

Copyright © 1991 by Schiffer Publishing Ltd.
Library of Congress Catalog Number: 90-62987.

All rights reserved. No part of this work may be reproduced or used in any forms or by any means—graphic, electronic or mechanical, including photocopying or information storage and retrieval systems—without written permission from the copyright holder.

Printed in the United States of America.
ISBN: 0-88740-286-0

This title was originally published under the title,
Bf 110 Zerstörer an allen Fronten 1939-1945,
by Motorbuch Verlag, Olgastrasse 86, 7000 Stuttgart 1.
ISBN: 3-87943-552-7.

We are interested in hearing from authors with book ideas on related topics.

Published by Schiffer Publishing, Ltd.
1469 Morstein Road
West Chester, Pennsylvania 19380
Please write for a free catalog.
This book may be purchased from the publisher.
Please include $2.00 postage.
Try your bookstore first.

Contents

Foreword	6
Wartime Rank Equivalents	6
Introduction	7
Chapter 1: The Early Years	9
History and Formation of the *Zerstörer* Units	10
The First Test — The Polish Campaign	33
Chapter 2: Action in the West and North	47
Air Battle over the German Bight	48
Operation "Weserübung"	54
The Western Campaign	76
Air Battle over England	90
Chapter 3: The War in the Mediterranean	119
Battle for Crete	120
Air War over Africa	145
Chapter 4: From the Arctic to the Black Sea	163
The Russian Campaign	164
War on Shipping in the Arctic	194
Chapter 5: Action over all Fronts	203
Defending the Reich	204
Afterword	247

Foreword

Free from pathos and overdone nationalism, this book portrays the everyday life of the *Zerstörer* units. Along with the accompanying text, the photographs portray the real, unfalsified situation of those times.

For that reason I wish this photographic documentation much interest and success.

Heinz Nacke, Major (Retired)
Knight's Cross holder and Squadron Commodore

Me 110 or Bf 110?

The type designations established in 1933 by the former RLM (Reichsluftfahrtministerium) consisted of an abbreviation for the name of the manufacturing firm and a (sequential) number, which was used only once.

The Messerschmitt-Werke AG was in business before July 1, 1938 as the Bayerische Flugzeugwerke, so that all Messerschmitt aircraft designs made up to that time bore the firm abbreviation "Bf":
Bf 108, "Taifun", low-wing sport and travel plane, Bf 109, most often-built single-seat fighter of World War II, Bf 110, heavy fighter introduced as "Zerstörer."

All later designs bear the firm abbreviation "Me", which has been applied popularly — though never officially — to the types listed above as well. In the technical literature, though, the correct type designation is used now as before.

The list below gives the equivalent wartime ranks of the Luftwaffe, RAF and USAAF

	Luftwaffe	Royal Air Force	US Army Air Force
1	Generalfeldmarschall	Marshall of the Royal Air Force	General (Five Star)
2	Generaloberst	Air Chief Marshall	General (Four Star)
3	General der Flieger	Air Marshall	Lieutenant General
4	Generalleutnant	Air Vice Marshall	Major General
5	Generalmajor	Air Commodore	Brigadier General
6	Oberst	Group Captain	Colonel
7	Oberstleutnant	Wing Commander	Lieutenant Colonel
8	Major	Squadron Leader	Major
9	Hauptmann	Flight Lieutenant	Captain
10	Oberleutnant	Flying Officer	First Lieutenant
11	Leutnant	Pilot Officer	Lieutenant
12	Stabsfeldwebel	Warrant Officer	Warrant Officer
13	Oberfeldwebel	Flight Sergeant	Master Sergeant
14	Feldwebel	Sergeant	Technical Sergeant
15	Unterfeldwebel	- No Equivalent -	- No Equivalent -
16	Unteroffizier	Corporal	Staff Sergeant
17	Hauptgefreiter	- No Equivalent -	Sergeant
18	Obergefreiter	Leading Aircraftsman	Corporal
19	Gefreiter	Aircraftsman First Class	Private First Class
20	Flieger	Aircraftsman Second	Private Class

Introduction

At the fighter pilots' meeting that takes place every October in Geisenheim, in which I took part every year, I met Mr. Herbert Schob. We talked, and Mr. Schob, of whom I learned that he held the Knight's Cross, promised to make his photographs from the war available for my archives. A week later it happened. I visited him in Frankfurt and was astounded when he gave me a whole trunk full of photo albums: photos, flight logs ranging from the birth of the Luftwaffe to its end — about its formation, the Spanish Civil War, the Polish campaign to the defense of the Reich, an almost complete documentation. When I saw this wealth of historical material, I first got the idea for this book.

This material, gathered in ten years of German air war history, provided me with a great opportunity to portray the development of a special genre within the Luftwaffe — the *Zerstörer*. It was of benefit to me that this aviator was there at the beginning and advanced from soldier to *Hauptmann* and Knight's Cross bearer, and had been able to preseve all his books through the turmoil of the war and the postwar era.

Meanwhile I was able to gain the cooperation of other *Zerstörer* pilots. Thus I can now present, along with my partner, Mr. Held, a unique work. From 1935 on, the birthdate of the German Luftwaffe, from the circumstances of its formation on to almost all fronts of World War II where Bf 110's were in action, this volume of pictures leads you. These pictures, privately owned and for the most part previously unpublished, provided a chronicle, documented in pictures, of the origin, effect and downfall of the Bf 110 in the Second World War. Photos of great technical as well as war-historical impact will give the reader information about the special form of combat that was the Bf 110. That they, at least after the Battle of Britain, were not up to their actual task of being heavy fighters was not the fault of the *Zerstörer* pilots. This responsibility belongs above all to the Luftwaffe command, the RLM and, not least, to the political leaders of those times.

At this point I would like to express my deepest thanks to the people and institutions who helped me assemble this book:

Hauptmann (Retired) Herbert Schob
Oberstleutnant (Retired) Hans Joachim Jabs, Commodore NJG 1, formerly ZG 76
Oberst (Retired) Wolfgang Falck, first Commodore of NJG 1, formerly ZG 76
Major (Retired) Heinz Nacke, Commodore ZG 101, formerly ZG 76
Horst Diener
Dr. Haupt of the Federal Archives, Koblenz

and many others. Above all, I would like to thank our publisher in Germany, Mr. Wolfgang Schilling, who gave us the chance to have our work published by his firm.

Naturally, one cannot, in the limited form of a single book, portray every moment exactly, nor is this volume meant to present the technical development or the historical sequence of the air war. It is meant to provide an overview and a first impression. Taken in this sense, this book offers the possibility of sharing in the experience of a genre of weapon from the formation and first years of the Luftwaffe to its end, as a piece of military aviation history.

The Author

CHAPTER 1

The Early Years

History and Formation of the Zerstörer Units
The First Test — The Polish Campaign

History and Formation of the Zerstörer Units

The concept of a "Zerstörer Unit" was developed by the command staff of the Luftwaffe for the first time in 1934. Göring was excited by this idea from the start. The concept envisioned a twin-engine plane with a crew of more than one, corresponding to a bomber in size and equipment, but carrying a particularly heavy armament instead of bombs. The advantage was supposed to be that the bomber could decrease its defensive weaponry for the benefit of its bomb load. Göring, who was fascinated by this idea, immediately instructed the Technical Department of the Luftwaffe to provide a description of this new type of plane. The Bavarian Aircraft Works, whose chief designer Willy Messerschmitt came closest to the Luftwaffe command's concepts with his design for the Bf 110, received the contract. And so the chronology of the development looked like this:

Beginning of airframe construction	Spring 1937
First complete Bf 110 A-0	August 1937
First flight of Bf 110 B-0	April 1938
Beginning of Bf 110 B-1 production	Summer 1938

Meanwhile the establishment of the first *Zerstörer* units took place — though, of course, with the Bf 109 C and D.

When World War II began on September 1, 1939, the following *Zerstörer* units were ready:

I./LG 1	Bf 110 C-1
I./ZG 1	Bf 110 C-1
II./ZG 1	Bf 109 E-3
I./ZG 2	Bf 109 D-1
I./ZG 26	Bf 109 C-1 & D-1
II./ZG 26	Bf 109 C-1 & D-1
III./ZG 26	Bf 109 D-1
I./ZG 52	Bf 109 D-1
I./ZG 76	Bf 110 C-1
II./ZG 76	Bf 109 D-1

As can be seen from this list, the majority of the units were still equipped with the Bf 109; when the war began, the available Bf 110's numbered only:

27 Bf 110 B-1
68 Bf 110 C-1

In 1939 only 156 Bf 110's left the factory in Augsburg. Particular difficulties in the development of this new weapon raised the question of suitable and powerful motors. The planned-for DB 601 was not available in sufficient numbers, so that temporary solutions had to be found. This delayed the delivery of large numbers to the troops.

The pilots were selected from the best pilots in the available fighter units, for this was to become an elite genre, the "Ironsides of the Luftwaffe", as Göring once said. That was, of course, an expectation that could never be fulfilled by the *Zerstörer* units, on account of their technical insufficiency and planning errors.

The Spanish Civil War then set new standards for the concepts of Luftwaffe leadership, so that only small numbers of the Bf 110 reached the units that were to use them before the war broke out.

Before we take up the actual establishment of the Bf 110 weapon, we should have a brief look at what went before.

When in 1935 the German Reich attained its full complement of military strength, and therefore air strength, the development of the Luftwaffe had already begun secretly. A small cadre of airplane pilots and flying personnel had been trained inside and outside Germany for the times to come. Thus the astonished public got the impression in 1935 that the new groups and squadrons of the Luftwaffe had emerged, as if out of nowhere, in the shortest possible time.

The newly established Luftwaffe was given a special priority in the formation of the Wehrmacht, a circumstance that was to reverse itself during the course of World War II. Scarcely any other arm of the Wehrmacht was as particular in choosing its personnel or trained them as thoroughly as the Luftwaffe. The pilots, most highly trained, were almost always capable of flying any airplane model available at the time.

The following chapter will treat these first years of training and the first tests.

In the first year of the rebuilding of an air force in Germany, many young aviators were sworn in, as here in Verden on December 12, 1936.

Here stands the later *Hauptmann* and Knight's Cross holder, Herbert Schob, as a proud young pilot.

Every beginning is difficult; Hans Joachim Jabs, later Kommodore and holder of the Oak Leaves, seems to be having a bit of trouble.

The Arado Ar 68 E was one of the last biplane fighters used by the troops.

The 6th Echelon and their Ar 65 planes transferred to a short-training airfield in the vicinity of Jüterborg-Damm on October 4, 1936.

Proper camouflaging is practiced during maneuvers at Jüterborg-Damm on October 4, 1936.

The aviation cadets were tested both with and without instructors, as here in Werl.

The first tests of the fledgeling pilots took place in these and other "mules."

Then the time came. The new pilots stood proudly before their Arado one-man fighters, in which they would now have their training as fighter pilots.

The farewell dinner with the instructional echelon of the 6th JG "Horst Wessel" at Werl on November 1, 1936. In the first row, from right to left, "Assi" Hahn, unknown, von Maltzahn, Mölders and Osterkamp.

After conquering their fears, the young pilots received their pilots' emblems as outward signs of their new dignity.

Scarcely had the motors cooled when new aviation cadets arrived.

Below: A cross-country flight in an Ar 66 C near Greifswald was part of navigation training.

The radiomen were trained in, among others, the Junkers Ju W 34 hau, as here at Waal in 1936.

Here we see a radioman in his seat in a W 34 hau.

Gradually the first fighter units were equipped with the new Bf 109 fighters; this one is a B-2.

The reequipping, carried out under great temporal pressure, led to many accidents. This was the Bf 109 B-2 of *Unteroffizier* Schob at Magdeburg on February 21, 1938.

Many lost their lives in flight accidents.

The guns of this Bf 109 B-2 are being adjusted anew.

While the pilots were already ready in their coveralls and flying helmets, the technicians were still there making their last adjustments.

A chain of planes flying low over the Baltic Sea toward the firing range.

Firing practice ranked among the mandatory and most important constituents of fighter-pilot training. Here a Bf 109 flies over the firing range after firing.

Below: We see the flight log of *Unteroffizier* Schob with his firing results written in.

In August of 1936 the first German pilots set foot on Spanish soil. They were the pilots of the Ju 52 transports and the six He 51 single-seat fighters which had flown Franco's troops from Morocco to Spain. With that, the young Luftwaffe faced its first great test. After the arrival of the transport echelons in August, the majority of the German units followed in November. Officially these consisted only of volunteers. In reality, though, they were ordered to Spain according to various criteria. This was done under the strictest secrecy, with constant changes of the personnel in Spain. The latter was done to give as many pilots and crews as possible the chance to gather experience at the front in this war. In strange uniforms, with strange emblems and under the name of the *Legion Condor*, German Luftwaffe forces fought in Spain from November 1936 to April 1939. A special staff of the RLM evaluated the experience gained there. It was to have its effect on the strategic and tactical concepts of the Luftwaffe during the beginning of World War II.

The Heinkel He 51 was the first fighter plane of J 88, the fighter unit of the *Legion Condor*, until replaced by the Bf 109.

When they appeared, the Bf 109's were far and away the most modern airplanes of their time. — A Bf 109 of the 2nd J. 88 in La Cenia, with the Spanish national emblem.

Units of the *Guardia Cevil* sometimes guarded the fighter planes of J 88 in Catania.

Unteroffizier Schob of the 2nd J 88 had to land this fighter away from the base because of lack of fuel.

A Bf 109 pack of the 2nd J 88 flying out of formation.

The Republican troops set up positions in the vicinity of Barcelona.

This machine was damaged by anti-aircraft fire during an attack on ground positions and had to crash-land.

The planes of a fighter echelon are repaired under the open sky.

The top hat was the symbol of the 2nd J 88 in Spain.

The "headquarters" of the 2nd J 88 at La Cenia in the summer of 1938.

This was the Bf 109 of Group Commander *Hauptmann* Gotthard Handrick. He won the gold medal in the Pentathlon at the 1936 Olympic Games.

The pilot of this Bf 109 with the Falange emblem gave it a bath near Tarragona.

Unteroffizier Schob's plane bore the letters NNWW as his personal symbol. The letters stood for "Nur nicht weich werden" (just don't get soft).

In June of 1938 a large part of the *Legion Condor* returned home. Here they parade in Hamburg before Luftwaffe Commander Göring and Legion Commander von Richthofen.

In the summer the Bf 110 B-1 went into production. It was meant to be used as a long-range fighter. It could never suit this purpose, though. The reasons could be found in faulty technical concepts.

The reorganizing or renaming of existing units to form the first *Zerstörer* units took place in the summer of 1938. They were generally equipped, though, with Bf 109 C and D planes, since technical faults and difficulties had appeared in the Bf 110 type, which had been designed and built especially for use in *Zerstörer* units. These difficulties mainly involved the supplying of motors. The supplying and, in fact, the manufacturing of suitable motors gave the responsible authorities problems, not just for Bf 110's and not just in 1938. This situation was caused by the lack of clear developmental concepts in the RLM and was never solved during the entire war. Thus it happened that only a very few *Zerstörer* units were equipped with the Bf 110 when they were established. In terms of personnel, the newly established units were composed of excellent pilots. Some of the pilots who had been decorated in the Spanish Civil War were also ordered to *Zerstörer* units. Thus the *Zerstörer* units were an elite group in terms of personnel, though not in technical terms.

On March 1, 1939 the 3rd Echelon of the I. ZG 76 was formed at the Fürstenwalde Air Base.

A Bf 110 of LG 1 at Barth. On the nose of the 110 is a wolf's head, the symbol of the I. LG 1.

The fighter and *Zerstörer* groups of Training Squadron 1 have all turned out for parade here. The groups were equipped with Bf 109 and 110 planes. L 1 was the code for LG 1. In this training squadron, Bf 110's and fighters as well as dive bombers and other planes were gathered and used for training and instruction.

The pilot of this Bf 110, *Oberfeldwebel* Schob, seen from the radioman's seat.

The shadow of another pack member shows up clearly on the left engine cowling.

Right: This is the seat of the radioman, *Obergefreiter* Landrock, in the Bf 110; the throat microphone is easy to see, as is the machine gun.

Several planes of LG 1 can be seen here at the Barth airfield.

Flying took place in almost any weather.

The MG 15 was the only defensive weapon to the rear and was used by the radioman.

The group adjutant and *Oberleutnant* Jäger talk with the technical officer, *Oberleutnant* Rademacher, and *Oberleutnant* Böhmel. On the Bf 110 one can see the adjutant's chevron at the left and the code M 8, that of ZG 76.

Firing practice became a constant part of the Bf 110 training program. Here one flies over the firing range.

Left: The first and at the same time probably the simplest test for the Luftwaffe was probably the occupation of what remained of Czechoslovakia. A swarm of Bf 110's passes over Vienna.

Bf 110's of the I. ZG 76 at Pachovice airfield in Bohemia. Bf 109's and 110's were still used simultaneously in the *Zerstörer* units then.

Bf 109 C planes of the I. ZG 76 have arrived at Pardubitz.

The Polish Campaign

When the war with Poland, and thus World War II, began on September 1, 1939, the following *Zerstörer* units were ready for the attack on Poland:

Unit	Commander	Planes	Air base
I. ZG 1	Major Huth	Bf 110	Muhlen
II. ZG 1	Major Reichardt	Bf 109 E	Friedberg
I. (Z)LG 1	Major Grabmann	Bf 110	Jesau
I. ZG 76	Hauptmann Reinecke	Bf 110	Ohlau
I. ZG 2	Hauptmann Gentzen	Bf 109 D	Gross Stein nr. Oppeln

Late in the afternoon of September 1, the German Bf 110's came upon some thirty Polish fighters over Warsaw. The I./LG 1, led by *Hauptmann* Schleif — the Commander, Major Grabmann, had been wounded in the morning — was then flying to escort the German units that were attacking Warsaw. *Hauptmann* Schleif discovered the Polish fighters among his planes and attacked. But the PZL fighters sensibly backed off. One of the Bf 110's seemed to have been attacked by the Poles. Slowly, steadily losing height, the plane slipped away. At once the Polish PZL 11's hung on her heels. But the seemingly badly damaged German plane led her pursuers toward her German comrades waiting nearby. At a range of eighty meters, *Hauptmann* Schleif fired on the enemies from the tail of the "broken-winged" 110. They repeated this trick four times until the Poles had had enough of it or had "smelled a rat." The result of this warlike trick was five planes shot down in a few minutes. On September 3 the Bf 110 again encountered thirty PZL 11 C planes over Warsaw. Again the group was able to shoot down five planes — this time without tricks. With that the group, with 28 attested scores, became the most successful air unit in the Polish campaign.

The actual assignment of the Bf 110's in the Polish campaign, though, was to attack supply lines and support the infantry. This was often necessary, for the fast advance of the German troops created dangerous gaps into which the enemy plunged. Along with dive-bombers and fighter planes, the Bf 110's had to stop the advancing enemies with bombs and guns.

Coming events cast their shadows. At the end of August 1939, all *Zerstörer* units of LG 1 were united at bases in the eastern part of the Reich. Here two Bf 110's are seen coming in to land at such a base.

The transport Ju, still painted in segmented camouflage, is loaded with supplies and spare parts.

Even while dressed in coveralls and felt boots, they found time for a fast round of Skat.

The technicians give the plane a last thorough check.

Before takeoff, the officers of the unit talk things over.

The Bf 110's of LG 1 are just lifting off from the field in chain formation.

This air parade, in which LG 1 took part, was officially a memorial procession over the Tannenberg monument in East Prussia (see the picture below). In reality, though, the squadron was moving to a new short-training base in the area of the advance route to Poland. The beginning of World War II was imminent.

On September 1, 1939 the Bf 110's joined the bombers and dive-bombers in an attack on Warsaw. Here the first air battles took place. *Feldwebel* Schob was able to record his first score in his flight book.

The Bf 110 C of *Feldwebel* Schob bears its first score mark next to the wolf's-head symbol of the I./(Z)LG 1.

The pilot and his radioman, *Obergefreiter* Landrock, proudly pose for the photographer.

The heavy weapons of the Bf 110 are more than a match for the Polish planes.

Here a PZL 11 that was just forced to crash-land is "pushed away."

Feldwebel Schob had more success over Warsaw. On the evening of September 5, 1939 he could apply his second score stripe.

The Bf 110's of ZG 76 also took part in the fighting in Poland. Here the I./ZG 76 is seen while still at their takeoff point in East Prussia.

Hauptmann Falck with several crews of his second echelon.

A Bf 110 of the 1st ZG 2 has noticed something suspicious in a patch of woods and heads down to attack.

A Polish artillery unit had hidden in the woods. They fell victim to the "Berneburg Hunters."

A short break between missions — from left to right: Rissmann, unknown, Stern and Schob.

A Bf 110 of the I. ZG 76 on a war-zone field in Poland.

The "black gang" of weapons and motor mechanics played a major role in the success of the air units through their tireless service.

Upper left: This plane's motor and landing gear were damaged in a low-level attack. Its one-wheel landing was a success, even though with "a little spin."

Lower left: A last inspection by the chief mechanic shows that the plane is cleared for action again.

The Bf 110's keep rolling to support the advance of the ground troops.

Planes of ZG 76 are seen here at Kielce airfield in the spring of 1940.

One of the modern planes of the Polish air forces was the very well-performing PZL 23. One of them is seen here at Radom airfield in April of 1940.

At this point — in the second week of the Polish campaign — camouflage was scarcely necessary. The Polish planes, after putting up a brave but hopeless fight, had disappeared from Poland's skies.

A Bf 110 echelon sets up in the middle of a cornfield.

The campaign against Poland, the first "Blitzkrieg" in history, has ended. At the Kielce airfield the Bf 110's are overhauled; these are planes of the I. ZG 76.

Hitler visits the *Zerstörer* pilots of the I. ZG 76 in Kielce. — From right to left: *Leutenants* Lent, Jäger, Rademacher and Gollob.

After the fighting in Poland ended, new *Zerstörer* units were established in Germany. This picture shows a Bf 110 of the newly formed ZG 26 at Dortmund in the winter of 1939-40.

CHAPTER 2

Action in the West and North

Air Battle over the German Bight
Operation "Weserübung"
The Western Campaign
Air Battle over England

The Air Battle over the German Bight

On December 18, 1939 the following *Zerstörer* units were subordinated to JG 1, commanded by *Oberstleutnant* Carl Schumacher:

Unit	Commander	Planes	Air base
I. ZG 76	Hauptmann Reinecke	Bf 110 C	Jever
II. ZG 1	Major Reichardt	Bf 110 C	1 echelon at Westerland, Sylt; 2 at Neumünster

On this day, 24 British Wellington bombers flew toward Wilhelmshaven. Just at this point, a test unit under *Leutnant* Diehl was stationed at Wangerooge. It was making tests with the new "Freya" radar device. So it happened that the British were discovered relatively early. But before the fighters arrived, the British had already flown over the Schilling roadstead and then Wilhelmshaven — but no bombs fell. As several captured British aviators later stated, they were only on a navigation run. Only as they were heading back, did the fighters and Bf 110's come upon the British unit. After a half-hour fight, a dozen English bombers of the Wellington type had been shot down by the I. ZG 76. Two Bf 110's, those of *Leutnant* Uellenbeck and *Hauptmann* Falck, had been damaged severely. *Leutnant* Uellenbeck and his radioman, *Unteroffizier* Dombrowsky, had been injured.

A few weeks later, on January 2 and 10, 1940, the I. ZG 76 was able to score further success against "Wellington" and Blenheim bombers.

Bombers of the Vickers "Wellington" type flew a navigation run that added with heavy losses for the Royal Air Force.

A radar device of the Freya type, like this one installed at Cap Nez, discovered the approaching British planes.

These listening devices were for a long time the only technical aids for early recognition of attacking enemy planes.

The 2. ZG 76, alerted by a report from surveillance, sets a course for the presumed approach course of the British.

Attack! A Bf 110 attacks "Wellington" bombers.

Smoking ruins on the North Sea mark the point at which a brave British crew died a senseless death.

While the plane of the group adjutant of the III. ZG 76 is already covered, an He 59 is still on its way to a sea rescue.

One of the "Wellington" bombers shot down in the battle over the German Bight.

Crews of the 2. ZG 76 — from left to right: Walz, Barnstorf, Trappiel, Zwickl, Kufka, Zinke, Lembke, Lentz, Held and Kaminski.

The Bf 110 of the echelon captain, *Hauptmann* Falck. The 2. ZG 76 used a ladybug as its emblem.

Jever, December 18, 1939: Pilots of the especially successful I. Group — in the front row, from right to left: *Hauptmann* Falck, *Leutnant* Jäger, *Leutnant* Gollob and *Leutnant* Lent.

A press conference was supposed to publicize the great success that the Luftwaffe had gained. *Oberst* Schuhmacher, the Commodore of JG 1, is seen here speaking with journalists; at his right is Reich Press Chief Dietrich, next to him *Hauptmann* Falck. At *Oberst* Schuhmacher's left it *Oberleutnant* Steinhoff.

Operation "Weserübung"

On March 28, 1940 the Allied war council decided to occupy neutral Norway. To prevent a threat to the north flank as well as the loss of sources of raw materials in Norway and Sweden, the Wehrmacht command in turn decided on an occupation. The following *Zerstörer* units took part in this campaign, which was given the misleading name of "Weserübung":

Unit	Commander	Planes	Air base
I. ZG 76	Major Reinecke	Bf 110	Westerland, Sylt
I. ZG 1	Major Huth	Bf 110	Westerland, Sylt

At 5:30 A.M. on April 9, 1940 the air offensive against Denmark and Norway began with the takeoff of the first transport units. But soon the first wave of Ju 52's, loaded with paratroopers and equipment, faced a fiasco. While Aalborg, in Denmark, was occupied by paratroopers without a fight, the units flying to Oslo-Fornebu with the X. Flying Corps, under *Generalleutnant* Geisler, were called back on account of bad weather. Thus it happened that only the Bf 110's of the 1. ZG 76, under *Oberleutnant* Hansen, were over the Norwegian airfield. Involved in heavy fighting with Norwegian "Gladiator" fighters, they eagerly awaited the paratroopers, but they did not come. Several of the Bf 110's had sustained shot damage already, and the first engines to be hit begin to smoke. What with the long flight and the subsequent heavy fighting, fuel ran low too. In this situation, *Oberleutnant* Hansen decided to land. He gave *Leutnant* Lent, whose Bf 110 was also hit and whose right engine was dead, the order to land first. The other Bf 110's flew over the field at right angles to Lent's approach course to keep down the numerous anti-aircraft and machine-gun positions with their weapons. *Leutnant* Lent did crash in this stormy landing, but he and his radioman were uninjured. Meanwhile the right motor of *Oberleutnant* Hansen's Bf 110 also died. He and the rest of the unit landed on their last drops of fuel. Meanwhile several Ju 52's of the second attacking wave arrived with infantrymen. Among these Ju's was the transport plane of the 1. ZG 76 with technicians on board. They busied themselves with the badly damaged Messerschmitts. Along

with the landed infantrymen, the Bf 110 crews mopped up the remaining nests of resistance. After that a proud radio report went out to the X. Flying Corps: "Oslo-Fornebu is in our hands — 1. ZG 76."

Farther north, additional Ju 52's with paratroopers on board were flying toward the Stavanger-Sola airfield. Heavy defensive fire made it impossible to land the fighters. At this moment two Bf 110's roared over the field and helf the anti-aircraft guns down with their 20mm cannons. They were two aircraft of *Leutnant* Gollob's 3rd Echelon, the only ones to arrive at Stavanger in the bad weather.

Oberleutnant Hansen was praised for his brave achievement by *Generalleutnant* Geisler personally several days later.

During the fighting at Stavanger a number of crews fell, including Major Reinicke, the Commander of the I. ZG 76.

This "Wellington" bomber was shot down on April 21, 1940 by Bf 110's of the 2. ZG 76 over Aggersund, Denmark.

The pilot of the RAF bomber, Flying officer F.T. Knight, has a cup of coffee with *Hauptmann* Falck — or is it tea?

Here Falck's chief mechanic adds another score stripe to the plane.

Hauptmann Falck and the symbol of the 2nd Echelon, a ladybug with its seven spots.

The last briefing before the mission.

In the strangely beautiful winter landscape near Aalborg, Denmark stands this Bf 110 of the I. ZG 76 in the winter of 1940-41.

The motors have to be warmed up before takeoff. The captain of the 2nd Echelon supervises this procedure personally.

The echelon provides an escort for Air Force Commander Göring, at left; to the right of him is *Hauptmann* Falck. In the row stand, from the top, Uellenbeck, Knötzsch, Fresia, Kalinowski, Walz, Lemke, unknown, Zwickl and Dombrowsky.

The base of the II. ZG 76. In the spring of 1940, life is still pleasant.

The echelon captain's Bf 110 is decorated with the echelon's flag.

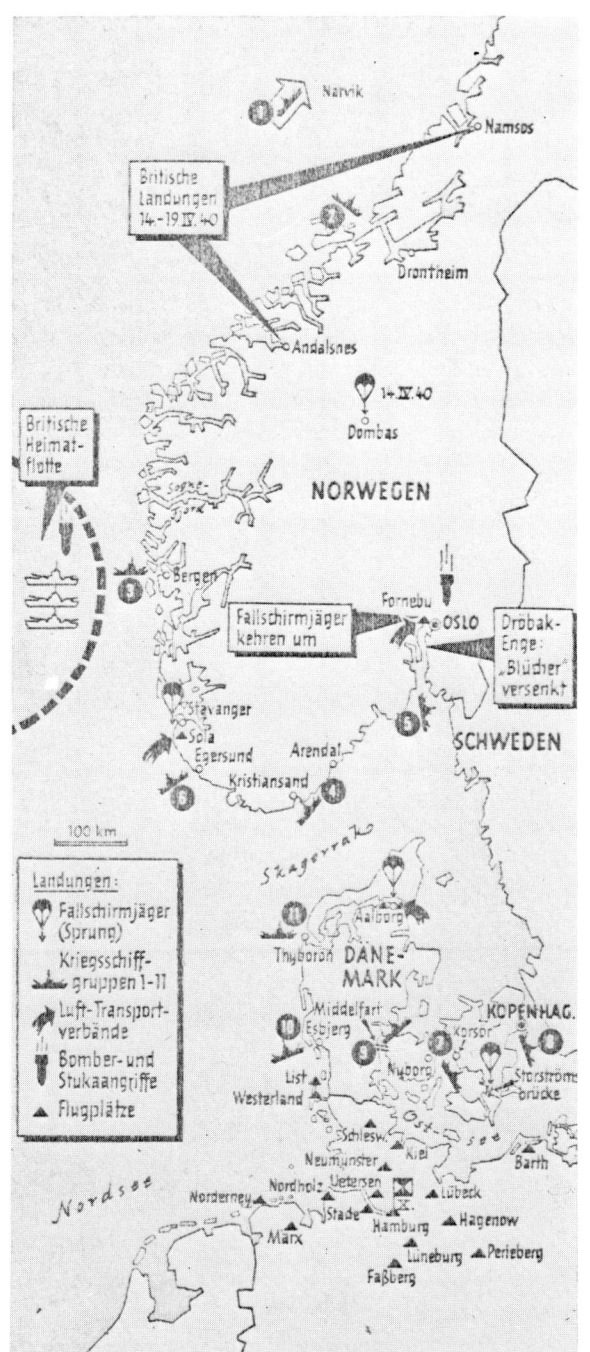

After Denmark had been occupied without a fight, the greatest combination of sea, air and ground forces in military history to that point set out. The Norwegian airfields were taken quickly from the air — some of them by Bf 110 crews of the participating Bf 110 units alone. The Norwegians, defending themselves bravely, were subdued from the air and the water.

Ju 52 transports bring paratroopers, weapons and supplies to Norway.

A Ju 52 over Sandnes approaches its assigned target.

A Bf 109 E escorts the transfer flight of the airfield operation company of ZG 76 from Westerland to Stavanger-Sola.

Leutnant Lent of the 1. ZG 76 crash-landed during the taking of the Oslo-Fornebu airfield.

The Stavanger-Sola airfield after being taken by German troops.

This Bf 110 of the 2. ZG 76 crashed during landing as a result of enemy fire. The Fresia-Barnstorf crew survived the scare.

Stavanger-Forus was another airfield bravely defended by the Norwegians.

New crews and planes have arrived from Germany. The Bf 110 D 1 has the special identifying mark of an auxiliary tank attached below the front of the fuselage. It was meant to increase the range but proved to be useless.

Here a new auxiliary tank is mounted. "Dachshund belly" was the nickname for these Bf 110's fitted with these tanks at Stavanger-Forus.

Tanking up — the Bf 110 D 1 gained in range but lost in fighting value because the plane became heavier and less mobile. In addition, the tank was not bulletproof and quickly caught fire when it was only half full.

Because of bad experiences with the "Dachshund's belly", fuselage and wing tanks that could be dropped were soon used instead.

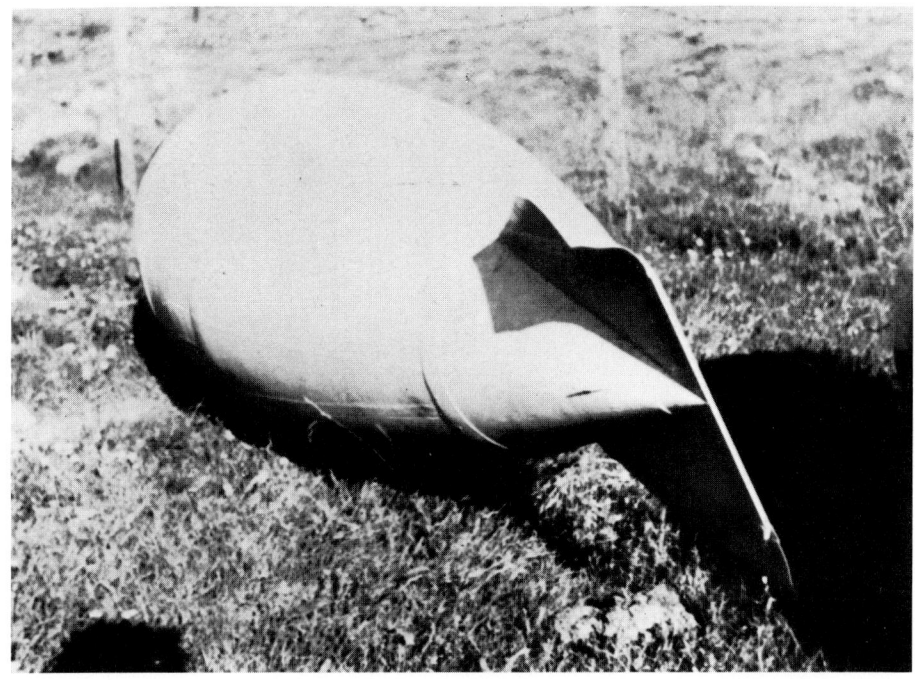

Bf 109 and Bf 110 side by side at the airfield in Stavanger.

The Bf 109 E of the echelon adjutant of the second group of the same squadron of JG 77. The picture was taken at Stavanger-Sola early in 1940.

The Bf 110 of *Oberfeldwebel* Fleischmann crashed while landing at Sola on April 30, 1940.

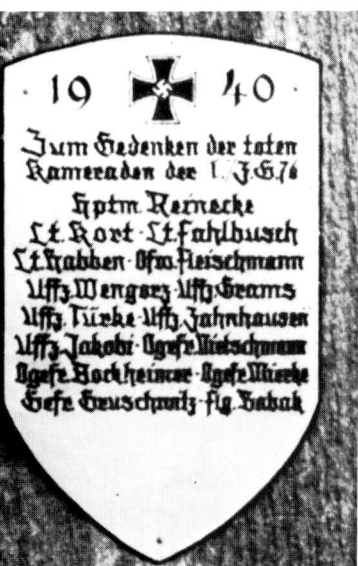

Many *Zerstörer* crews were lost during and after the first fighting in Norway. At Stavanger-Sola the I. ZG 76 erected a memorial stone to their fallen comrades in front of the staff building.

A bullet in the motor forced the pilot of this plane to break off his attack on a "Blenheim" unit.

A new motor is installed; the last few twists of the wrist finish the job.

The Trondheim airfield seen from the air. Bombers, destroyers and fighters were based here.

A Ju 88 parked at the edge of the field was set afire by British Blenheim bombers.

The He 111's of Battle Group 100 were not hit.

Messerschmitt Bf 110's patrol above the Trondheim Fjord and wait for a reported British torpedo-bomber unit.

This Blackburn "Skua", a dive bomber of the Royal Navy, attacked the German battleships lying in Trondheim Fjord on June 13, 1940. It was shot down at 2:02 P.M. by the crew of *Oberfeldwebel* Schob and *Obergefreiter* Pape.

Under the protection of the Bf 110's in Norway were a German battleship, other heavy units, destroyers and transport ships.

The usual picture seen by the pilots in the cockpit of the Bf 110 every day.

Here is the radioman's workplace. The radio sets can be seen particularly well, as can the drums of 20mm ammunition for the plane's guns.

Bf 110's were to be found at almost all the focal points. Here a plane is flying over the Tromso Fjord.

There was rarely a break. Planes sitting quietly, like this Bf 110 of the I. ZG 76 at Oslo-Fornebu, were the exception in the early days.

The "black gangs" were constantly on duty to keep the planes of the two *Zerstörer* groups in action in the Norwegian campaign in operation.

The Norwegian mountains form an unforgettable background for the base of the I. ZG 76 at Stavanger-Forus in April of 1940.

Imagination knew no bounds in the creation of unit emblems. Above, I. ZG 52; right, I. ZG 2; below, I. ZG 26.

The Western Campaign

After France and Britain had declared war on Germany, absolutely nothing happened at first. The so-called "sitting war" lasted from October 1939 to May 10, 1940. This date had been set by Hitler for an attack in the west.

The following *Zerstörer* units stood ready for service in the west at this time:

Unit	Commander	Base
Staff ZG 26	Major Huth	Crailsheim
I./ZG 26	Major Mackrocki	Crailsheim
II./ZG 26	Hauptmann von Rettberg	Gelnhausen
III./ZG 26	Major Schalk	Bönningshardt
I./ZG 1	Hauptmann Falck	Düsseldorf
Staff ZG 76	Major Grabmann	—
II./ZG 76	Major Groth	Nellingen
I./ZG 2	Major Gentzen	Lachen-Speyerdorf
V.(Z)/LG 1	Major Rubensdorfer	Würzburg
I./ZG 52	Major Lessmann	Schorndorf

Over Holland, as well as on the ground at its air bases, the Bf 110's disposed of a great number of enemy planes in the first days of the western campaign. On May 14, 1940 Holland capitulated, after being first to be attacked in the west. In their further course of action, the Bf 110's showed their first serious defects in battle with French fighters, for the aircraft used as fighters were too slow and not maneuverable enough. When Britain then intervened in the Battle of France with fighter planes of the Hurricane and Spitfire types, it became clear that the Bf 110 was not suited to use as a fighter. This became very obvious in the massed air battles between British fighters and German Bf 110's during the fighting over Dunkerque.

At the break of dawn on May 10, 1940 the Bf 110's of ZG 26 prepare for action.

The "shark group", the II. ZG 76, attacks the enemy's supply routes as instructed. The war had now flared up in the west too.

A swarm of the 6. ZG 76 flying out of formation here in the Sedan area.

Oberleutnant Jabs in his plane, M8+NP. At this time he had already scored six victories.

In the first days, the British tried in vain to stop the German advance from the air. This is how a German artist envisioned the dramatic events in the air.

But the battle did not leave the Messerschmitt Bf 110's unscathed. Here the right motor, which has been hit, is replaced.

With a combined score of 41, the 6. JG 76 and their leader; from left to right, *Oberleutnant* Jabs, Echelon Commander *Hauptmann* Nacke and *Oberleutnant* Herget.

The Group Commander of the II. ZG 76, *Hauptmann* Groth, second from right, sits with his officers here in France in May of 1940.

A swarm of the 2. ZG 26 files to meet a pack of British bombers.

This Wellington was forced to land after it had tried in vain to attack a German tank unit.

These Bf 110's fly low as they approach a French air base near Metz.

The French Air Force was destroyed on the ground to a great degree, as in the case of this Potez 63 II light bomber.

A quick takeoff for the 2. ZG 76. The crew, *Leutnant* Uellenbeck and *Unteroffizier* Dombrowsky, gets into their plane. Unlike the pilots, who wore seat parachutes, the radiomen enjoyed the greater mobility of the back parachute.

The left motor of this plane has "gone sour."

The crew of this Bf 110 had to crash-land, and their plane burst into flames and burned out.

Hauptmann von Rettberg, Commander of the II. ZG 26, discusses a mission with his men here. The "wooden shoe" was the emblem of the group.

Well camouflaged is half survived. This saying was also true of this Bf 110 of the 5. ZG 26 near Lille, early in June of 1940.

The Bf 110's of the II. ZG 26 return together from an attack on airfields in the Paris area to their base at Grecy, early in the summer of 1940.

A successful crew proudly tells the men on the ground about their mission.

The staff swarm of the II. ZG 76, with *Hauptmann* Groth leading, turns aside to attack ground targets near Paris.

This plane had to crash-land because of shot damage, and the chosen field turned out to be too short.

Despite heroic resistance, the French Air Force — some of it with modern equipment — came to grief, badly led, most of the planes were destroyed on the ground.

The Bf 110's of the II. ZG 76 fly over the destroyed city of Dunkerque, symbol of the British defeat.

Destroyed tanks and trucks as well as bombed ships remain after the British withdrawal.

The Bf 110's of the I. LG 1 also took part in the great victory parade of the German troops in Paris.

The Air Battle over England

After the great successes of the Polish campaign as well as the action in Norway and France, the moment of truth for the Bf 110's approached now in the "Battle of Britain." Over Great Britain, the North Sea and the Channel, the new aircraft were to be shown the limits of their potential. Conceived as a long-range fighter, the Bf 110 first raised doubts as to its suitability for that task during the French campaign, for there they encountered not outmoded types of planes, as in Poland, Holland or Norway. Now their opponents were modern fighters of the Hurricane or even Spitfire type. While the Bf 110 might have been able to hold its own against the Hurricane, it actually needed fighter protection against the Spitfire. It could no longer be counted on to carry out its actual task of protecting the bombers. More and more often the Bf 110 pilots had to save their own skin by flying a defensive circle. Thus they were useless as active fighter escorts. So this newly conceived weapon could not handle its role as a fighter over Britain. Many crews paid for this error of the Luftwaffe command with their lives, their health or their freedom. It must be pointed out that the Bf 110's did win aerial battles again and again. For example, on one day ZG 26 shot down 52 enemy planes while losing only twelve of their own.

The following *Zerstörer* units had been gathered in the west in August of 1940 to fight against Britain. Some of these units would no longer exist after this decisive conflict. For example, the I. ZG 52, which was completely wiped out during escort missions over England.

Unit	Commander	Base
Air Fleet 2	Generalfeldmarschall Kesselring	Brussels
Jafü 2	Oberstleutnant Osterkamp	Wissant
Erpr. Gr.210	Hauptmann Rubensdörfer	Calais-Marck
ZG 26 Staff	Major Huth	Lille
I.	Hauptmann Mackrocki	Yvrench
II.	Hauptmann von Rettberg	Crecy
III.	Major Schalk	Barley
ZG 76 Staff	Major Grabmann	Laval
II.	Hauptmann Groth	Abbéville
Air Fleet 3	Generalfeldmarschall Sperrle	Paris
Jafü	Oberst Junck	Deauville
ZG 2 Staff	Major Vollbracht	Toussée le Noble
I.	Hauptmann Ott, then Heinlein	Amiens
II.	Hauptmann Carl, then Lehmann	Guyancourt
LG I V (Z)	Major Liensberger	Alencon/Caen
	then Peters	Vaerloese
Luftflotte 5	Generaloberst Stumpff	Stavanger
I. ZG 76	Major Restemayer	Stavanger

The echelon of the II. ZG comes in to land at their base in Abbéville before a bad-weather front.

The first Bf 110's of the I. ZG 52 roll out to take off. They are to escort the battle groups of Air Fleet 2 in their missions against England.

With motors roaring, one Bf 110 after another lifts off. Target: Meeting point with the bombers.

In the row formation typical of fighters, the Bf 110's take their course toward England.

This "balloon killer" belongs to the III. ZG 26, which was at St. Aubin in mid-September 1940.

A Bf 110 picked up this heavy slug in a low-level attack on British light anti-aircraft guns.

Dramatic moments in the life of *Oberfeldwebel* Birndorfer's crew of the 6th Echelon of ZG 76. Just short of the English coast, *Ofw.* Birndorfer had to crash-land in the water with a shot-up left motor. The daring maneuver succeeded. After a neat landing, the plane stayed afloat long enough for the pilot and radioman to escape.

The radioman of this Bf 110 receives replacement drums for the 20mm cannon.

The Bf 110 of *Unteroffizier* Fresia of the 2. ZG 76, the "Ladybug Echelon", took off from Aalborg for an attack on Britain. Additional tanks made this long-distance flight from Denmark to England possible.

The 2nd Echelon flying over Harwich, on the east coast of Great Britain. The auxiliary tanks have already been dropped.

The first Bf 100 flies over the English coast.

A Bf 110 has spotted the well-camouflaged British airfield and dips his wings to attack.

A Bf 110 of ZG 26 over Bexhill, a town on the south coast of England.

Before the well-camouflaged quarters of the 2. ZG 76, *Unteroffizier* Fresia (at left) tells his comrades of his mission.

The stomach also wants its share. Between missions, the crews take their meals quickly and in flying clothes.

A swarm of Bf 110's returns across the Channel from a mission to England.

This Bf 110 pilot has had a rear-view mirror mounted — a trick that he surely learned from the British fighter pilots.

Leutnant Viktor Mölders was a *Zerstörer* pilot for a long time before he joined the squadron of his famous brother Werner.

After takeoff, a swarm of the II. ZG 76 takes formation over their base in Abbéville and sets a course for the coast. The *Zerstörer* missions became more and more costly; more and more frequently, crews did not return from their missions.

Back from a mission.

An exhausted *Oberleutnant* Borchers climbs out of his Bf 110 after a mission against London.

Oberleutnant Jabs has returned after a costly mission. He himself was successful, but more and more often, comrades were lost over England.

Oberleutnant Herget, left front, and *Oberleutnant* Jabs, right, discussed the aerial battle over England from which they have returned. *Hauptmann* Nacke, Commander of the 6. ZG 76, was wounded and has his arm in a sling. In the background stand, at left, *Unteroffizier* Moorweiser, *Oberfeldwebel* Egger's radioman, and at right, *Unteroffizier* Weissflog, *Oberleutnant* Jabs' radioman.

On October 1, 1940 *Hauptmann* Groth, the Commander of the "Shark Group", and *Oberleutnant* Jabs received the Knight's Cross. The picture shows them after their return from the awarding in Berlin.

The brand new holders of the Knight's Cross.

Hauptmann Groth with his Knight's Cross wearers Jabs and Nacke. *Hauptmann* Nacke, Commander of the 6. ZG 76, received the Knight's Cross on November 2, 1940.

A Bf 110 at Abbéville in the summer of 1940. The "shark's mouth" was the well-known symbol of the II. ZG 76.

A Bf 110 crew gets aboard their plane. The motors are already running.

The planes have taken off in a row. Their course leads to England.

The sleek Messerschmitt's quickly gain altitude.

At the coast the twin-engine fighters meet the Heinkel bombers.

The individual swarms head for the coast.

A conversation around the water trough — Abbéville, July 1940; seated from left to right are Groth, König, Hohbein, Weber and Jabs. Nacke can be seen standing behind Groth with his arm in a sling.

The command post of the II. ZG 76 in Abbéville.

A distinguished visitor to the *Zerstörer*. Major Grabmann, Commodore of ZG 76, greets *Generalmajor* Osterkamp, fighter-pilot leader on the Channel, who strides by briskly.

Oberleutnant Jabs with his Bf 110 in the winter of 1940/41.

Feldwebel Weissflog, *Oberleutnant* Jabs' radioman, became a night-fighter pilot himself, an *Oberleutnant* and a holder of the Knight's Cross toward the end of the war.

A Bf 110 of the 5. ZG 76 flying back from a mission over southwestern England.

More and more often, Bf 110's did not return. These three were lucky.

109

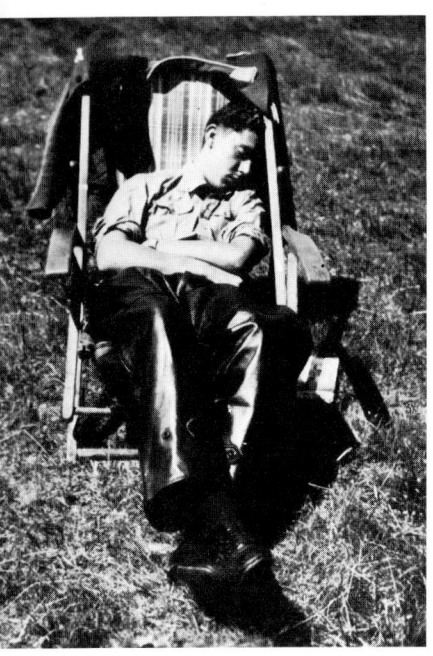

The missions became harder and harder for the pilots. A nap between missions, here taken by *Oberleutnant* Jabs, became a necessity.

The 6th Echelon tasting wine at Le Mans in 1940.

The camouflaged hangars of the 6. ZG 76 at Le Mans in the late summer of 1940. From left to right: Borchers, König, Herget, Jabs and Nacke.

Like the pilots, the planes undergo a hard test of durability. Constantly the "black gang" must keep working to keep the planes ready for service.

Technical servicemen — without them, the success of the flight personnel would have been unthinkable.

The "shark group" has well-known guests from the sports qorld. Between Major Groth, the Group Commander, at right, and *Hauptmann* Nacke, Commander of the 6th Echelon, stand motorcycle racing champion Ernst Henne, left, and racer Hans Kilian.

Hauptmann Nacke shows Hans Kilian the score stripes on the fin of his Bf 110.

While the German Luftwaffe fought a hopeless battle over England, a landing in England was practiced on the beaches of France.

Rebuilt Rhine ships were to be used as transport and landing craft.

This is how they imagined the trip across the Channel. These pictures show how halfhearted Hitler's preparations for a landing in Britain were.

Scarcely one Bf 110 came back undamaged — if it has the good fortune to come back at all. This Bf 110 "doing a headstand" belonged to the I. ZG 52, which was completely wiped out over England.

A service in the early autumn of 1940 for a crew from the II. ZG 76 that crashed on landing as a result of shot-up landing gear.

This Bf 110 returned from a mission over London badly damaged. It is the plane of Group Commander *Hauptmann* Groth, who had been lucky again.

Flying low over the water to shake off the pursuing British fighters, this Bf 110 reached the French coast.

The units were not able to carry out the assignment given them. Wrongly conceived technically, the Bf 110 could not be used to carry out actual fighter assignments despite the courage and sacrifice of their crews. The Battle of Britain made this abundantly clear. Action that might have been aimed at eliminating the technical faults of the "heavy fighters" was never taken by the RLM.

Despite high losses, the *Zerstörer* continued to carry out their mission of escorting their own bombers, though they themselves needed fighter protection.

While the Bf 110 crew is taken prisoner in England, their plane burns in the background.

CHAPTER 3

The War in the Mediterranean

Battle for Crete
Air War over Africa

The Battle for Crete

The Italian move against Greece in October of 1940 placed the German leadership in the unfortunate position of having to help its ally Italy. In a countermove to the Italian attack on the Balkans, the British moved into Greece and also occupied Crete and Malta as important Mediterranean support points. In this situation, Hitler ordered the "Mercury" action, the conquest of Crete from the air, on April 24, 1941. On May 20, 1941, 7:05 A.M., the attack began with a bombardment by all available forces of the small town of Malemes and its airfield on the seacoast, as well as Hill 107, which dominated the whole surrounding area.

Zerstörer units took part in Operation "Mercury" with the following units:

Unit	Commander	Base
Staff	Major Schalk	
I. ZG 26	Hauptmann Mackrocki	Argos
II. ZG 26	Hauptmann von Rettberg	Argos
II. ZG 76	Hauptmann Groth	Argos
III. ZG 76	Hauptmann Kaldrack	Argos

Above all, the Bf 110's had the task of knocking out the British anti-aircraft positions as well as the connecting routes between the main defense areas of the British and Greeks. Thus, for example, the road from Suda Bay, where the English landed their supply ships, to Chania was constantly attacked by the Bf 110's of the II. ZG 76. The anti-aircraft positions were centered around the island's three airfields. The mountain hunters were to be dropped at these three airfields by Ju 52 planes.

The airports of Malemes, Reythmnon and Iraklion, though, had been expanded to major defense points. Thus the paratroopers suffered heavy losses, since they jumped in the midst of the English who were ready for them. The Bf 110's of ZG 26 and ZG 76 had to clear the way for the hard-fighting paratroopers. Thus not only the anti-aircraft positions and supply routes, but also the artillery positions, fortified defensive positions and the like were constantly attacked by the Bf 110's.

The II. ZG 76 on a transfer flight to the Balkan front.

A stopover is made on a Bulgarian airfield.

In what language is this conversation with the Bulgarian aviators being held? *Hauptmann* Nacke seems to have found the right words — as the smiling faces show.

Hauptmann Nacke and his Bulgarian fellow officer have exchanged pilot's emblems.

What might this Bulgarian herdsman think of the modern warplanes behind his back?

Hauptmann Nacke has his boots polished in Sofia.

Planes of the II. ZG 26 take off for Yugoslavian airfields at the first light of day.

One after another, He 111 bombers and Bf 110 take off on their missions.

On a quickly prepared airfield in the Balkans, bombs are brought to the planes by oxen.

The ZG 26 on an airfield in northern Greece in November of 1940.

Oberfeldwebel Schob views the Acropolis in Athens. The Balkan campaign is over.

But there is no rest. The crews are being familiarized with their new assignments.

Meanwhile the planes are thoroughly overhauled.

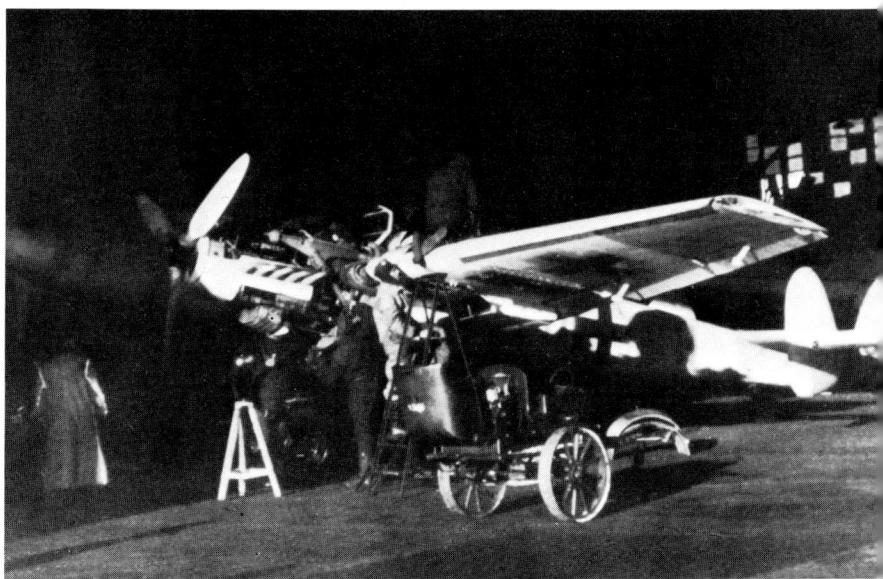

Additional squadrons and groups, such as the II. ZG 76, are transferred to Greece.

During the transfer, the II. ZG 76 takes a break at Belgrade airport; from left to right: *Hauptmann* Groth, *Oberleutnant* Borchers, *Hauptmann* Nacke, *Oberleutnant* Jabs, *Oberleutnant* Herget and *Leutnant* Schmud.

Meanwhile the dependable Ju 52 carries the equipment southward.

The "shark group" reaches the Aegean Sea.

Over the former Greek capital of Nauplia, Bf 110's fly from the south to their new base at Argos.

Plane after plane lands on the deserted airfield at Argos.

No trees cast a shadow here.

Oberleutnant Jabs eats his pea soup at 37 degrees Celsius. Will the table last much longer?

After a refreshing storm, the mechanics get to work; here we see ZG 26, which was also based near Argos.

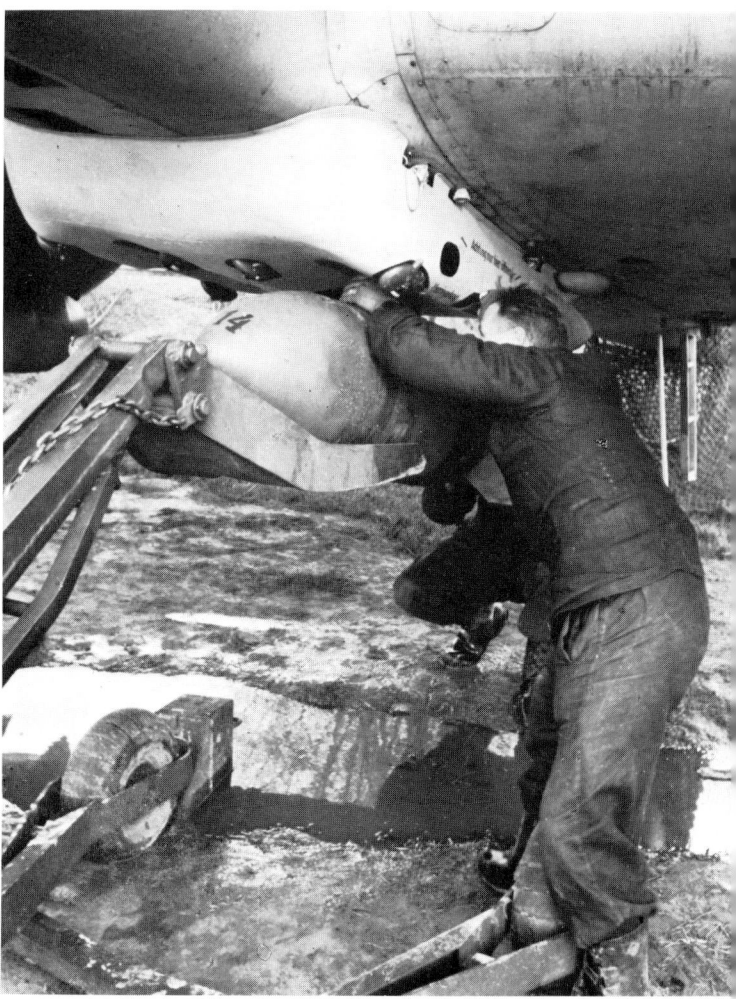

The motors are tested one last time before the date set for the attack, for it will be a long way over the sea.

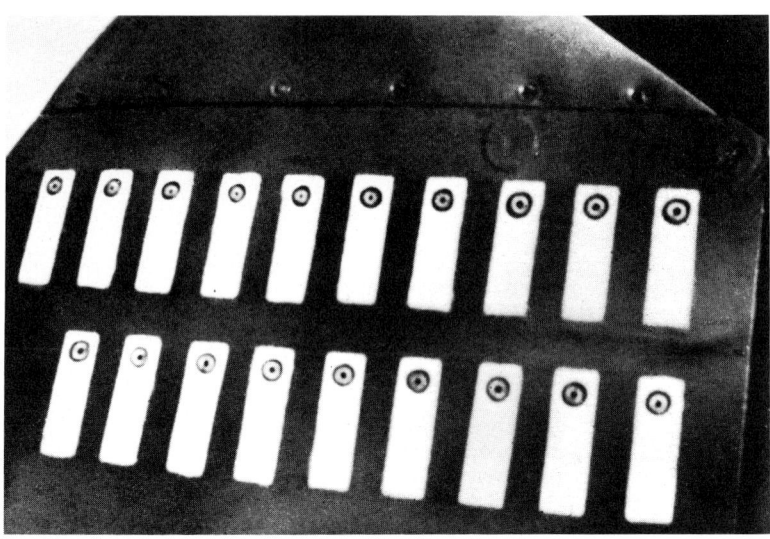

The tail of *Oberleutnant* Jabs' Bf 110, with his 19 score stripes.

Heinz Nacke visits Hans Joachim Jabs at Argos.

The first units fly over the Greek coast toward Crete. The attack on the island begins.

Out over the water, the Bf 110's carry their deadly loads toward the island, which is occupied by the British.

Over the harbor of Rethymnon, Crete's capital, the first columns of smoke rise, caused by bombs that have struck.

While bombers, dive-bombers and Bf 110's try to bombard Crete in force, the transport planes are loaded at the Greek takeoff points. This Ju 52 has a 37mm antitank gun slung beneath it.

Paratroopers in their typical overalls, also known as "bone bags", and with their rimless jumping helmets, wait for the command to get aboard.

Then Operation "Mercury", the occupation of Crete by air, begins. Wave after wave of Ju 52 transports flies over the sea to Crete.

The command to jump rings out. For many it is a jump to death.

The paratroopers jump in close order. Fearful, seemingly endless minutes on the parachute begin now, in which the paratroopers are delivered to the enemy, defenseless. Many die in the air.

While the paratroopers jump, the Bf 110's try to knock out anti-aircraft and machine-gun positions.

A Bf 110 flies low over a British position.

For the paratroopers who have survived hanging defenseless from their parachutes and the first dangerous minutes on the ground while unhooking their chutes, a merciless battle now begins.

A merciless man-to-man fight begins amidst the buildings.

More and more Germans are buried in Cretan soil.

Bf 110's attack positions at Chania.

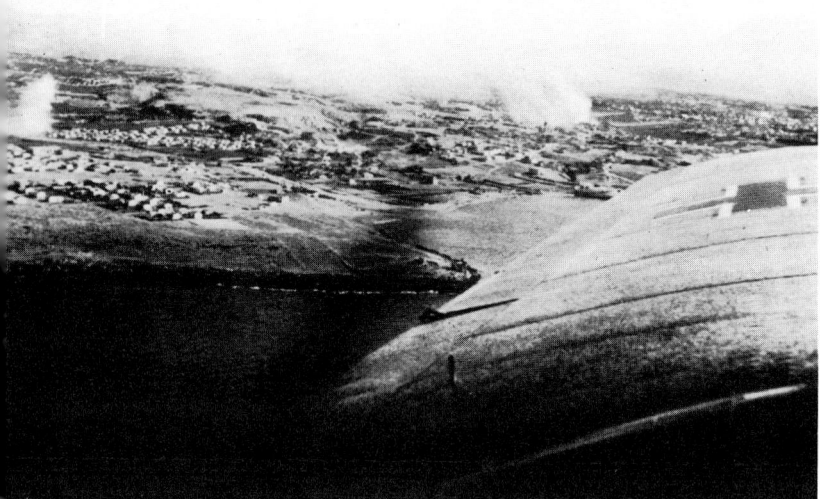

As they fly over Chania and out to sea, the numerous fires in the city can be seen.

The airfield of Heraklion is still in enemy hands.

The hotly contested airfield of Malemes is scattered with the wrecks of Ju 52 transports that landed in enemy fire, brave to the end.

Again and again Bf 110's of the II. ZG 76 attack the British positions.

The road from Chania to Suda Bay, a main supply route, is under fire from Bf 110's.

Suda Bay — from here the British tried to move their supplies inland. Many of the ships fell victim to the German dive bombers.

Bf 110's also suffered increasing losses, usually from infantry weapons.

In ceaseless attacks, the planes naturally suffer much damage. Mechanics are replacing a motor here.

Weapons mechanics are on hand to prepare ammunition for the machine guns and fill the drums for the 20mm cannons.

Crete has fallen. The III. ZG 26 has begun to set up various takeoff points on Crete.

The survivors of the III. ZG 26 go to air bases in Sicily. In the background is Mount Etna.

The *Zerstörer* units take up new tasks in the Mediterranean area. They are to move against the British in Africa. Here a plane of ZG 26 takes off.

The Bf 110's of the III. ZG 26 escort sea transport to Africa.

A Bf 110 passes a Ju transport on the way to Africa.

The Air War over Africa

The fact that Hitler and his General Staff Chief Halder always regarded Africa as merely a minor theater of war became known after the fact. So it came about that the high command only accomplished minor goals in the Mediterranean area. This is all the more surprising in that Crete was captured with great sacrifices of men and materials in order to be able to attack Africa and the Suez Canal more effectively. Thus the underestimation of the African war zone by the German leadership found expression in the technical and personal supplying of the *Afrika Korps*. It is no longer surprising that only a single *Zerstörer* unit, the III. ZG 26, was stationed in Africa. It not only had to support the battle groups in their attacks on British targets, but also to intervene constantly in ground combat. And that was not all — it also had to undertake escort duty for the sea and air transport units coming over the Mediterranean. The III. ZG 26 was based in Gazala in the spring of 1941. The takeoff point for flights over the Mediterranean was Derna, where the Ju 52 transports coming from Sicily arrived as well. The assignments changed constantly; sometimes ships or transport planes had to be protected from the British who operated out of Malta, then the *Zerstörer* units took part in bombing attacks on Malta and the British convoys coming to it.

In Africa Bf 110's flew many missions against Tobruk and other ground targets. The fighting over the sea and the desert was costly for the III. ZG 26. Their Commander, Major Kaschka, fell in an aerial battle over Bir el Gobi on December 4, 1940. Almost a year later his successor, *Hauptmann* Steinberger, met a pilot's death.

Despite their small numbers and the great material and personnel problems they had to deal with, the *Zerstörer* units accomplished a great deal in the Mediterranean area. One must keep in mind the numerous assignments they were given and the great distances over which the Mediterranean theater of war spread.

A *Zerstörer* group under Major Kaschka was given an insoluble problem. The Bf 110's were outnumbered and overpressured to meet escort and combat assignments simultaneously. Thus particular praise is due to the calmness with which the small number of Bf 110 crews went at these overwhelming tasks.

Tense and alert, the radioman follows the reports on enemy activities.

Bf 110's reconnoiter the sea lanes from Sicily to Tunis.

This Bf is visited by a tank of the *Afrika Korps*.

An Italian Fiat G 50 fighter accompanies the Bf 110's. The question is who is protecting whom!

The brotherhood of arms is demonstrated for the photographer over the desert. A Macchi C 200, a Bf 110 and a Fiat CR 42, from top to bottom, fly in chain formation.

An evening scene at an airfield in Tunisia — late in 1940.

The "staff tent" of the III. ZG 26 in Derna — spring 1941.

Native nomads visit the crews in order to trade.

A convoy is met by the Bf 110's of the 8th Echelon of ZG 26.

Two Bf 110's fly low over their proteges.

Tripoli is reached at last, and the convoy is safe.

An especially hotly contested fortress was Fort Bir Hacheim, which was defended by the French. Bf 110's constantly attacked the supply lines to the fort.

A chain of Bf 110's flies over a German supply unit on their way to the front.

The impressive takeoff of a *Zerstörer* echelon from Derna airfield.

While the bombs explode on the ground, Bf 110's attack the enemy positions with their guns.

A Bf 110 of Reconnaissance Group 14 had to crash-land after being hit by anti-aircraft fire.

A Messerschmitt of the same unit has just returned from a reconnaissance flight. The camera is quickly removed and the film taken out.

This Bf 110's cannons are being taken out for repairs. It is a plane of the 9. ZG 26 "Horst Wessel."

Repairs under the open African sky — changing an engine in a field workshop of ZG 26.

A Bf 110 of the 8th Echelon after takeoff, on its way to the sea to locate a reported British convoy.

A Bf 110 of the same unit flies to meet a dive-bomber group and escort it.

This plane of the staff of the III. ZG 26 has flipped over while landing.

This Bf 110 takes off to join dive bombers on a joint mission.

A nomad tribe visits the desert base of a *Zerstörer* echelon.

The 8. ZG 26 "Horst Wessel" takes over the escorting of the Ju 52 transporters.

Feldmarschall Kesselring was the supreme commander of the German troops in the southern sector of the European theater of war.

Cramped quarters were always the rule at Derna when another transport flight made it across the sea; in the foreground are unloaded barrels of fuel, as well as two Bf 110's.

These Bf 110's are already loaded with bombs. It was customary to wear life jackets during missions over the North African coastal area.

A Bf 110 swarm flies over the Via Balbia, the main advance and supply route of the *Afrika Korps*.

Some planes advanced as far as the Pyramids of Gizeh. A wer correspondent who experienced this advance as a gunner added this drawing to his report of the mission.

This plane belonged to the 2nd Echelon, which was soon assigned to support the decimated III. Group.

The air bases in Africa all looked the same. Among half-wrecked Fiat biplanes stand the Bf 110's of ZG 26.

Two Bf 110's of the "Horst Wessel" Squadron fly over a sentry boat of the Navy in the Aegean Sea.

Like the Bf 110's of the II. ZG 76, the RAF pilots have painted shark mouths on their Kittyhawks.

On February 12, 1942 the battleships "Scharnhorst" and "Gneisenau", the heavy cruiser "Prinz Eugen" and other ships broke through the English Channel. Strong fighter and *Zerstörer* units were assigned to escort them. The photos show Bf 110's of ZG 76 passing destroyers of the naval kind and flying over the battleships.

CHAPTER 4

From the Arctic to the Black Sea

The Russian Campaign
War on Shipping in the Arctic

The Russian Campaign

At the beginning of 1941, despite all of Hitler's glorious predictions, Britain was not yet beaten. On the contrary, Britain had begun an offensive in North Africa against Germany's chief ally, Italy.

Under these conditions, Operation "Barbarossa" — the Russian offensive —began in the eastern part of the Reich. The following *Zerstörer* units took part in it:

Unit	Commander	Planes	Base
2. ZG 76	Oberleutnant Brandis	Bf 110	Kirkenes
Staff SKG 210	Major Storp	Bf 110	Radzyn
I. SKG 210	Hauptmann Stricker	Bf 110	Radzyn
II. SKG 210	Hauptmann Kaldrack	Bf 110	Radzyn
Staff ZG 26	Oberstleutnant Schalk	Bf 110	Suvalki
I. ZG 26	Hauptmann Spiess	Bf 110	Suvalki
II. ZG 26	Hauptmann von Rettberg	Bf 110	Suvalki

The 2./ZG 76 became the 1.(Z)/JG 77 (autumn 1941), then the 10.(Z)JG 5 (spring 1942), then the 13.(Z)/JG 5 (summer 1942).

The Bf 110's of SKG 210 that saw service in the area of the II. Flying Corps of Loerzer, as well as the *Zerstörer* units of ZG 26 fighting in the area of the VIII. Flying Corps under von Richthofen, specialized chiefly in destroying the Russian air forces on the ground. This changed during the course of the campaign. When the Soviets broke through at various points, the *Zerstörer* units were often called in as "firefighters", in which the ZG 26 often stood out.

The SKG 210 in particular could show a record to be proud of. Nearly a thousand planes, thousands of motor vehicles, two hundred fifty tanks and a great number of locomotives were destroyed by it. Also on its score were some eighty batteries with about 200 guns.

At the end of September parts of SKG 210, and then the whole unit, were withdrawn from the eastern front. In August of 1941 the I. and II. ZG 26 were transferred home for refreshment, and the last echelon followed in the spring of 1942.

Thus there were no more *Zerstörer* units stationed in the southern and central sectors of the eastern front at that time. Only in the far north did a single echelon remain. Only as of the spring of 1942 were the newly established squadrons ZG 1 and ZG 2 again in operation on the eastern front.

On June 22, 1941 the Russian campaign began. The Bf 110's, like those of the II. ZG 26 seen here, took off for action against Russian airfields.

The Messerschmitts of the 2nd echelon of the "Horst Wessel" Squadron fly toward their designated target.

This a war correspondent's view of Bf 110's attacking a Russian airfleid.

A downed Il 2 of the Russian air forces.

With these veterans of the Spanish Civil War the Russians tried to fight off the German Luftwaffe. But like these I 15's, most of the Russian planes were destroyed on the ground.

A swarm of the II. ZG 26 flying to intercept a Russian air unit reported by intelligence.

Scan the skies with your eyes — that's what *Oberfeldwebel* Schob is doing.

A Russian plane could be shot down.

At the beginning of the Russian campaign, all *Zerstörer* units in the area of the Army Group Center, or Air Fleet 2, were subordinated to *Generalfeldmarschall* Kesselring. So it happened that a number of *Zerstörer* officers were always at hand for command discussions in that area: from left to right, Major Trautloft —JG 54; *Oberstleutnant* Schalk — ZG 26; at right with RK *Hauptmann* Spiess — ZG 26; with his back to the camera, General Keller.

Hauptmann Spiess was the Commander of the I. ZG 26 at the beginning of the Russian campaign.

Major Trautloft and *Hauptmann* Spiess discuss a joint mission in front of the staff building of JG 54.

Hauptmann Theodor Rossiwall, Echelon Captain of the 5. ZG 26, receives the Knight's Cross from the hands of *Generaloberst* Keller on August 6, 1941.

After the conferring, from left to right: *Generaloberst* Keller, *Hauptmann* Rossiwall, General Förster, *Oberstleutnant* Schalk, Commodore of ZG 26.

ZG 26 fought on many fronts. This "flag parade" gives impressive evidence of that.

Hauptmann Thierfelder was Commander of the II. ZG 26 at the beginning of the Russian campaign.

Ice and snow often made service at the east-front airfields impossible.

When someone dared to take off anyway, he risked total failure, like this Bf 110 of ZG 1's "Wespe Squadron."

What do you do with a Bf 110 lying on its back?

Already equipped with winter camouflage, this plane is fueled — Russia, central sector, winter 1941-42.

The engines are started.

A Bf 110 slid off the icy runway after landing.

Oberfeldwebel Schob has scored his tenth victory.

The successful Schob proudly presents his "bookkeeping."

Hauptmann Thierfelder drinks to the success of his group.

Another occasion to celebrate is a crew's 200th combat mission.

A bomb attack is planned. The bombs, of 50 and 250 kg calibers, are already at hand.

With the help of a bomb lifter, the 250-kg bomb is hung under the fuselage.

S 9 was the code for SKG 210, a *Zerstörer* unit formed especially for the Russian campaign.

A curious collection: Bf 110, He 111 and Ju 87.

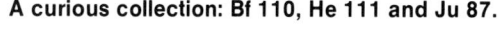

The Bf 110's, like their single-engine colleagues, had a string of successes to report in the Russian campaign: 12 score stripes on the tail of this Bf 110.

The Russian air force lost a great number of planes on the ground.

But the Bf 110's had to accept losses too, such as these damaged and crash-landed planes of ZG 26.

Bf 110's of ZG 26 attack a Russian tank unit.

This crew had to crash-land their plane because it was hit in the engine. The picture was taken just after landing.

A bomb just missed this tank but set it afire.

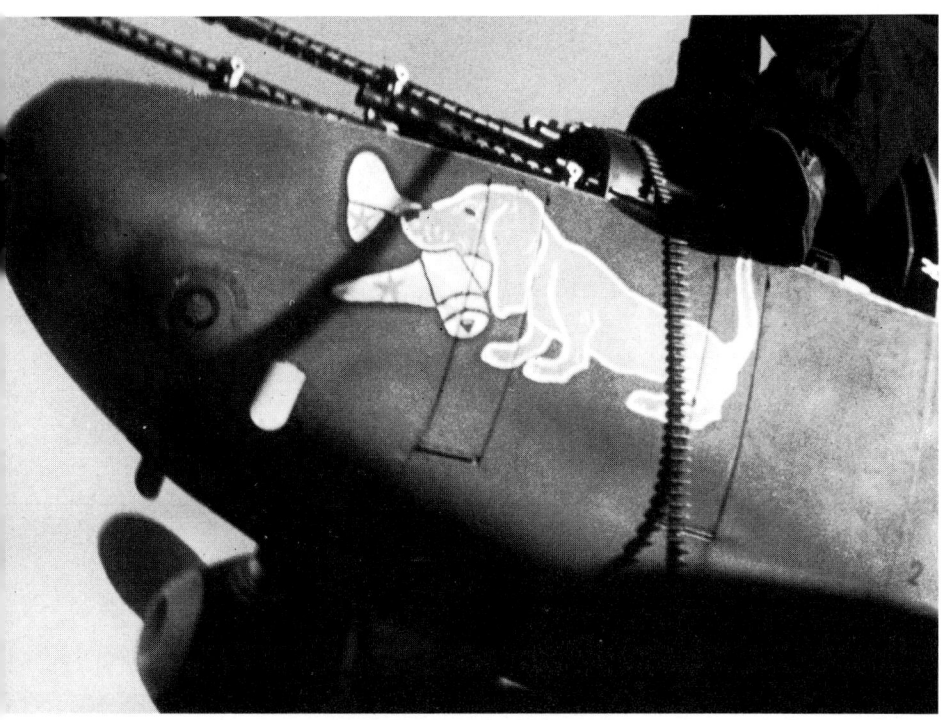

The emblems of several *Zerstörer* units during the Russian campaign:

Left: 10. (Z) JG 5 "Dachshund Echelon"

ZG 1 "Wespe Squadron"

Left: Replacement *Zerstörer* Group

Right: ZG 26 "Horst Wessel"

A Bf 110 dips its left wing to attack a spotted target.

The striking "face" of a Bf 110.

Oberfeldwebel Schob of the II. ZG 26 sits in his plane, ready to take off on command.

One of the reported Russian fighters of the Il 2 type flies over the base.

At the same moment, the alarm pack takes off.

A plane shot down south of Bryansk on January 9, 1942.

A new mission awaits. The crews of the II. ZG 27 go to their planes.

A quick check of the map.

The planes of the II. ZG 26 fly toward their target, a Russian tank unit.

Without the tireless service of the technicians, the success of the *Zerstörer* units, and of the entire Luftwaffe, would have been impossible.

The pictures show the engine and propeller of a Bf 110 of ZG 26 being changed.

A swarm of Bf 110's in the central sector of the eastern front flies to intercept a reported Russian tank unit.

Fw 190 fighters take care of protection.

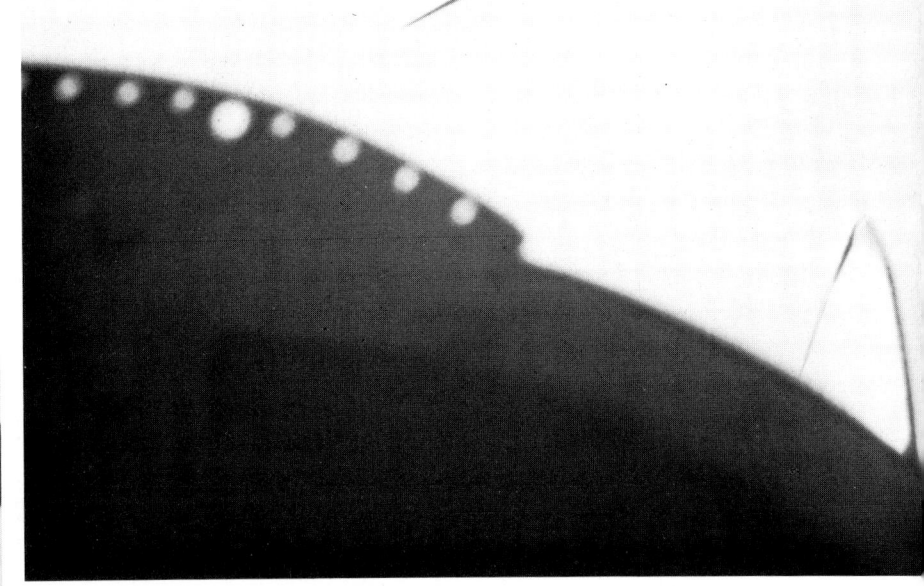

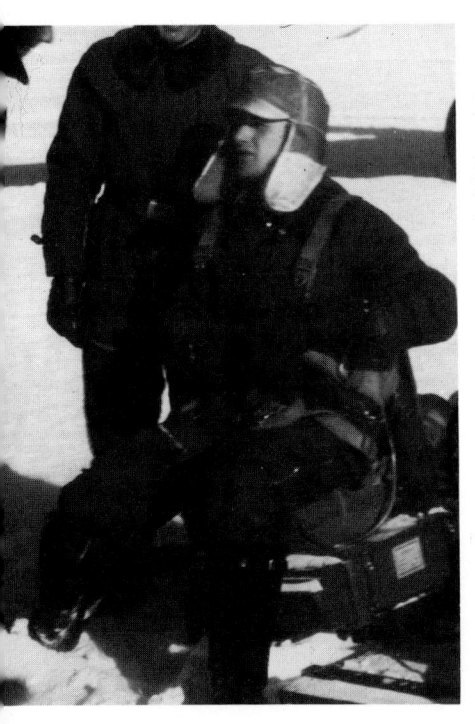

With his parachute still on, *Hauptmann* Thierfelder must sit down and report on the mission.

April 1942 — *Hauptmann* Schürmann reports to General of the Fighter Pilots Galland on his arrival at Deblin-Irena, where a new *Zerstörer* replacement group was set up.

The Bf 110's of the new unit carried the 4 M code. At the left and right front they bore a huge wolf's head, the former symbol of the I. LG 1.

Ready for takeoff, the Siebel Fh 104, General Galland's travel plane, bears the wolf's head of the *Zerstörer* units, as well as other fighter squadron emblems.

Bf 110's of ZG 1, with the wasp as their symbol, fly over the Dniepr.

A shot-down Bf 110 in Russia in the summer of 1942.

A plane of the "Wespe Squadron" is loaded with bombs. The crew prepares for a mission — Byelgorod, July 1942.

As they approach their target, Bf 110's fly over a Russian village.

The few Bf 110's on the eastern front were "maids of all work": heavy fighters, light bombers or reconnaissance planes — whatever was needed.

Bf 110's of ZG 26 at the Russian air base near Orsha —Autumn 1942.

Damaged by anti-aircraft fire, *Oberfeldwebel* Schob's Bf 110 crash-landed just short of the base after a long flight on one motor.

Oberfeldwebel Schob receives the German Cross in gold.

The II. ZG 26 takes off together, carrying bombs for use against a Russian breakthrough.

The Ju 88, like this C-6 seen in the Mediterranean area in 1943, was also used as a destroyer.

To deceive enemy bombers, a glass nose was painted onto this Ju 88 C-6. Thus from a distance it looked like the Ju 88 bomber, from which one need not fear a fighter attack.

The Ju 88 C-6 was used as a destroyer and night fighter. The latter can be recognized by the two bulges on the front of the fuselage to hold the "antlers."

War on Shipping in the Arctic

In 1940 only the 2nd Echelon of ZG 76 remained at Stavanger after the withdrawal of almost all *Zerstörer* units. In 1941 it, commanded by *Leutnant* Brandis, was transferred to Herdla. At the beginning of the Russian campaign the 2. ZG 76 was subordinated to JG 77 in Kirkenes as the 1.(z). Soon after that the echelon got its name of "Dachshund Echelon." This was shown in the echelon emblem. It was named for the three dachshund mascots of the echelon, "Herdla", "Lockheed" and "Bamse."

The echelon's chief assignments were as follows:
1. Escorting bombers and dive-bombers in their attacks on the harbor and city of Murmansk.
2. Attacking the Murman Railway leading inland from Murmansk.
3. Fighting off enemy bomber attacks on German or Finnish army units.
4. Protecting German ship convoys in the Arctic.
5. Attacks on Allied convoys going to Murmansk.

On March 16, 1942 the 1.(Z) JG 77 was renamed the 10.(Z) JG 5, then on June 26, 1942 it became the 13.(Z) JG 5.

This situation remained until July 18, 1944, when the echelon was detached from JG 5 and became the 10th echelon of a newly formed IV. ZG 26. Its first commander, *Oberleutnant* Brandis, was killed on February 2, 1942 after an attack on the Murman Railway; on his way back, he crashed in a bad-weather front. He was succeeded by *Oberleutnant* Schlosstein, then *Oberleutnant* Kirchmeyer and finally *Hauptmann* Treppe in that capacity. The latter then became the Commander of the IV. ZG 26.

A Bf 110 E of the 1.(Z) JG 77 over the Arctic Ocean.

The 1.(Z) JG 77, the "Dachshund Echelon", used its mascot as an emblem on the nose of its Bf 110 E planes — Kirkenes, August 1941.

A Bf 110 coming in to land.

The "black gang" did their work devotedly everywhere, as here in the Far North.

Oberleutnant Ziegenhagen has landed. An unusual look at the "roof" of a Bf 110.

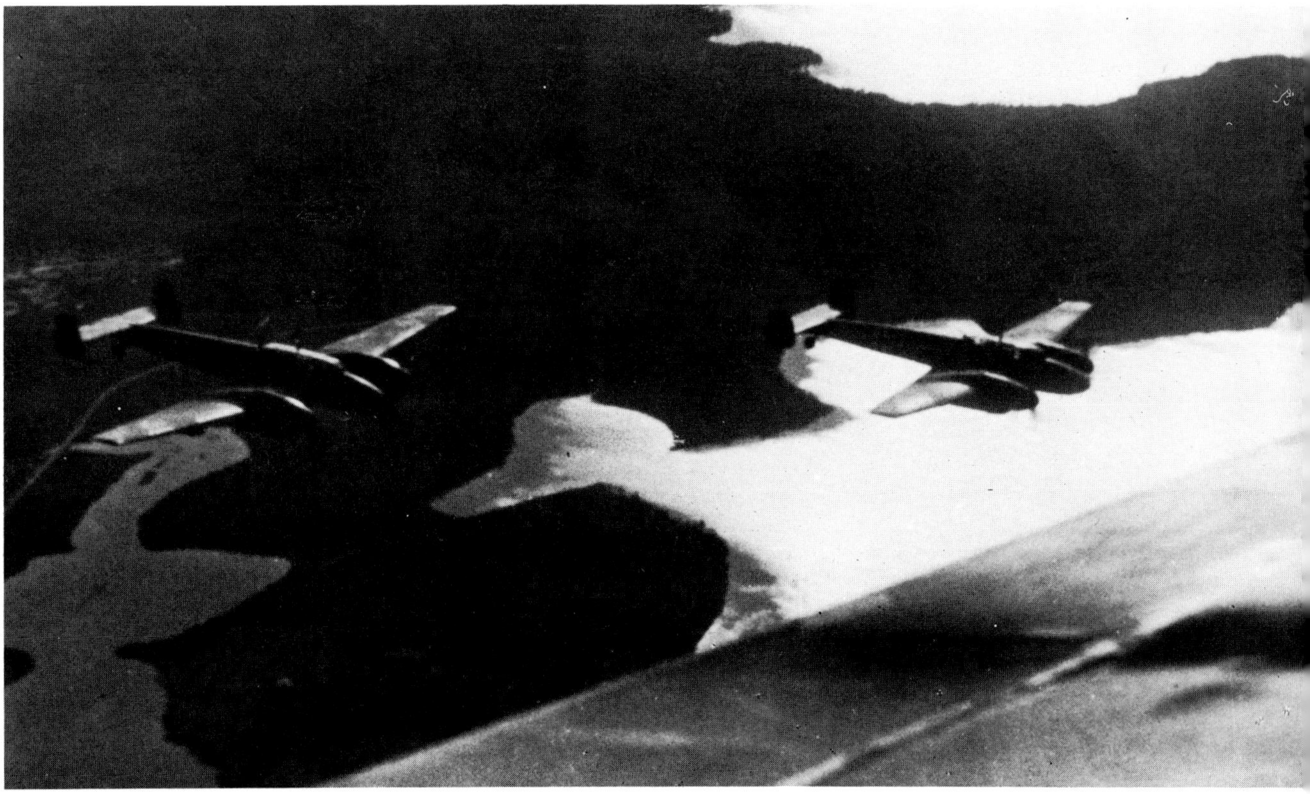

Two Bf 110's fly over the Finnish lake district.

A Bf 110 is on duty escorting a German convoy.

Only the Bf 110 D's of the "Dachshund Echelon", with the help of their extra fuel tanks, could operate effectively over the Arctic Ocean.

Kemi airfield in northern Finland — located on the Gulf of Finland right at the Swedish border.

An honored guest of the 10.(Z) JG 5. The Chief of Air Fleet 5, *Generaloberst* Stumpff visits the *Zerstörer* echelon. The second from right is General Roth, *Fliegerführer* of Lofoten.

The comrades of the single-engine fighter unit of JG 5 in Kirkenes.

A Bf 110 had to crash-land in the winds of northern Finland because of shot damage. The skid marks in the snow are clear to see.

Again and again the Bf 110's take off to escort the fighters on their attacks against the Murman Railway.

The harbor and air base at Kirkenes have the same importance in supplying the German troops fighting in Lapland that the harbor of Murmansk has for the Russians. Russian bombers attack the air base at Kirkenes again.

This plane, 1B+LX, is flown by *Oberleutnant* Ziegenhagen.

Bf 110's of the "Dachshund Echelon" provide an escort for the He 111's in their attack on Murmansk harbor.

Oberleutnant Brandis, at right, was the Echelon Captain of the 10.(Z) JG 5 for a long time. At left is radioman Feldwebel Baus.

CHAPTER 5

Action on All Fronts
Defending the Reich

Defending the Reich

After the entry of the United States into World War II, the British, who had been waging the air war against Germany alone, gained support in increasing quantities. While the British flew only night attacks, the B 17's of the 8th USAAF came in the daytime. Those Bf 110's that had not yet been transferred to night fighting flew along with the single-engine fighters against these streams of bombers. Efforts were made to counteract the lack of speed and mobility in the Bf 110 with heavy armament. This armament included not only additional machine cannons under the fuselage, but also the 21 launcher devices under the wings and their 21-cm rockets. On August 17, 1943, several swarms of Bf 110's made an attack against 376 B-17 bombers that were attacking Schweinfurt and Regensburg. Thanks to the greater range and explosive power of the rockets it was possible to fight the bombers outside the range of their enormous armament, and to score a series of victories. At least the detonating shells had the effect of scattering the packs. However, Bf 110's never again played a decisive role in combat. The few units that had not yet been converted for night fighting were disbanded bit by bit. The pilots were retrained for the single-engine Bf 109 and Fw 190 fighters. Thus great portions of Fighter Squadrons 300 to 302 were recruited from former *Zerstörer* pilots. What remained of *Zerstörer* Squadrons 1, 26 and 76 were still flying against the Flying Fortresses at the end of 1944.

The II, ZG 1 was stationed in northern Italy in 1944; its Commander, Major Nacke, was visited by an Italian staff.

The Italians showed a keen interest in the interior of this Bf 110 of the II. ZG 1.

A swarm of the 5/ZG 1 flies to intercept an American bomber unit reported from the south.

The USAAF began the strategic air war against Germany and the territories occupied by it from England in 1943. At the beginning, the main carrier of this battle was the American B 17 bomber. This plane was photographed shortly after dropping its bombs; its bomb bays are still open.

On the Channel coast, anti-aircraft units have opened fire on returning American bombers.

In March of 1944 *Oberst* Handrick visits ZG 76.

Oberst Handrick reviews the guard of honor; at left is the Commodore of ZG 76 at that time, Knight's Cross bearer Major Kowalewski.

Crews of the II. ZG 76 have gathered in front of a heavily armed Bf 110 G-2.

The auxiliary tanks of a Bf 110 are filled.

These Bf 110's are in action as pack destroyers. As additional armament, they carry two 21 launcher devices (WG 21) under their wings.

The plane of *Oberleutnant* Schob is ready to take off; under the cabin is his personal symbol, NNWW (nur nicht weich werden), that he used since the Spanish Civil War.

A swarm of heavily armed Bf 110's flies toward a reported American bomber unit. Their armament consists of two MG 151 in the floor of the fuselage, two MG 151 in the belly pan, one movable MG 81 Z at the rear of the cabin, four WG 21 launchers under the wings.

This was the enemy. An American combat box of B 17 Flying Fortresses.

Thus one can imagine the conflict between Bf 110's and the bombers.

On November 28, 1943 a serious accident took place in the 3. ZG 76 at Graz. On account of an icy landing strip, two planes slid off the runway shortly after touching down and rammed already landed planes. After the accident, four Bf 110's had to be written off.

Attempts were made with ever-heavier armaments, such as that of this Bf 110 G-2/R-4 (2 MK 108 and one 37-mm Flak 18, one MG 81 Z) to take on the heavily armed bombers.

The Bf 110's of ZG 76 await the enemy over the Alps.

A swarm of the 1. ZG 76 approaching Salzburg on April 16, 1944.

The main assignment of the heavily armed Bf 110 before 1944 was, among other things, scattering the American bomber packs. The scattered bombers were then supposed to be easy targets for the fighters defending the Reich.

A group of the III. ZG 76 answers the alarm and takes off.

The planes of the 6. ZG 76 set their course for a group of B-17 bombers of the 8th USAAF.

The American bomber group is already under anti-aircraft fire.

Bf 110's intercept the bombers over the Alps.

A view of the bombers as seen over the wing.

The overly heavy armament of the Bf 110 is supposed to make the difference.

The hunt was successful. Despite high losses of their own, Bf 110' continued to score new victories.

...berkommando der Luftwaffe
Chef f. Ausz. u. Diszpl. (V)
Az. 29 Nr. 519 /44

Berlin, den 1o.9.44.

An 1./Z.G.76

Der 1./Z.G.76

wird der Abschuß eines amerikanischen Kampfflugzeuges vom Typ

Boeing " Fortress II "   am 6.3.44, 12.38 Uhr

durch Oblt. S c h o b

als dreizehnter (13.)   Luftsieg der Staffel anerkannt.

I. A.

Mechanics of ZG 26 mount a shot camera.

Lest instructions to the III. ZG 26 before takeoff.

One after another, the Bf 110 planes take off from the runway, while the next machines taxi up.

Loading the launcher tubes of the WG 21 with rockets was a hard job and demanded fingertip sensitivity.

Four-engine bombers of the B 24 "Liberator" type attack a German hydrogenation plant near Hannover. While the first gas tanks are burning, the heavy anti-aircraft guns keep firing.

Oberleutnant **Schob is among many planes in the vicinity of the Americans and attacks.**

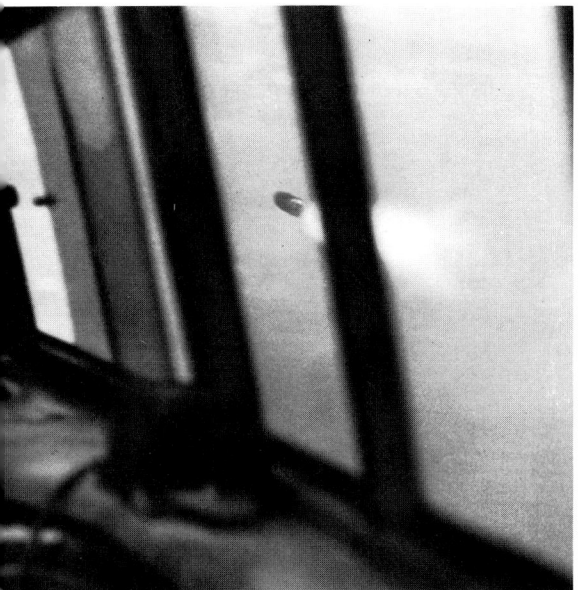

A WG 21 salvo — a rocket is shown shortly after leaving the launcher — drives the bomber group apart.

This B 24 has been driven away from its pack.

Under the fire of the Bf 110's heavy armament, the outer port engine has come to a stop. As a sign of the assignment, the American pilot has deployed the landing gear.

But despite the hard-fought victories, the stream of American bombers does not stop. Accompanied by hundreds of fighters that charge like dogs around a herd, the bombers of the 8th USAAF, sometimes thousands at a time, stream toward Germany day after day.

The Me 210 was supposed to replace the totally outmoded Bf 110 in the troops. But a series of misfortunes caused the Me 210 to be withdrawn from troop use even after it had gone into production. Frequently occurring flat spins were one of the main reasons.

By lengthening the fuselage and making other changes, the Me 410 was developed. A swarm is seen being flown to its new unit.

Other than a more powerful motor, the Me 410 also had a considerably improved panoramic view than the Bf 110.

The new "mule" is examined by a curious *Hauptmann* Schürmann.

The face of the Me 410.

The pilot's seat.

The radioman's seat. The controls for the two machine guns at the right and left sides of the fuselage can be seen clearly.

At the end of October 1943 the *Zerstörer* Replacement Unit at Deblin-Irena was renamed the 1. Battle Squadron 152. At the same time, its Bf 110's were replaced by Focke-Wulf 190's; Me 410's were added later. The first commander of the new battle group was Major Druschel.

4M was retained as the code for the new battle group, as was the wolf's head that dated back to LG 1.

An Fw 190 A-3 if the 1. SG 152 being serviced at Deblin-Irena.

This plane belongs to the same unit.

Future Bf 110 pilots at flight school in Memmingen were trained on the Arado 96.

A *Zerstörer* replacement unit, led by *Oberleutnant* Schob, was based at Ohlau.

So many crashes at Ohlau show the difficulty of becoming a good pilot.

Oberleutnant Schob greets the *Generaloberst* with his staff on his arrival at Ohlau.

On June 9, 1944 *Oberleutnant* Schob was awarded the Knight's Cross from the hands of *Generaloberst* Stumpff.

Along with *Oberleutnant* Schob and two other generals, *Generaloberst* Stumpff inspects the guard of honor.

After 500 combat missions and 28 aerial victories, six of them in Spain, *Oberleutnant* Schob is awarded the Knight's Cross.

Oberstleutnant Kowalewski led ZG 76 from February to August of 1944. In November he became the Commodore of the newly formed KG 76, which flew Arado 234 jet bombers.

Major Kaminski commanded the II. ZG 76 in the defense of the Reich from October 1943 to August 1944.

Weapons mechanics belt cannon ammunition.

An Me 410 over Germany in the autumn of 1944.

General of the Fighter Pilots (General der Jagdflieger) Galland visits ZG 76 at Seerappen in the late autumn of 1944.

Talking with *Zerstörer* pilots; from right to left, Galland, Handrick, Müller Trimbusch, Adjutant von Galland, Schob.

On the occasion of this visit, the assembled crews were informed that destroyer flying was being halted. The existing units were being transferred to fighter squadrons for day fighting.

Pictures taken at Königsberg in November of 1944 — this particularly heavily-armed version of the Me 410 belonged to the II./ZG 26. Note the aiming scope.

B 17 bombers bombard the freight yards in Koblenz. The drawn-in lines mark the location of the depot.

Christmas 1944 — former *Zerstörer* pilots and fighter pilots are united.

A Christmas card of the *Zerstörer* type.

Two fighter aces visit the "retired *Zerstörer* pilots"; from left to right, Gerhard Thyben, Anton Hackl.

This idyllic summer scene does not show the true situation of the Luftwaffe in 1944-45.

Only individually do former Bf 110's, used now in a fighter role, get into combat.

Till the end, the technicians do their responsible and indispensable work. These Me 410's are stationed in East Prussia in February of 1945.

Hauptmann Schob (center), along with *Oberleutnant* Ziegenhagen, explains the air situation report at Seerappen in 1945.

Major Kaminski, at right, having a bit of refreshment.

A particularly good picture of the Me 410 at Seerappen in 1945.

Opposite page:
Above: A large number of the remaining Me 410 units stayed on the ground in 1945 for lack of fuel.

Below: Only rarely did the staff swarm of the II. JG 76 take to the skies with their twin-engine fighters in the battle for Germany.

As here at Menningen, base of ZG 101, which had formerly been a flight school, the German airfields were destroyed in a hail of bombs.

An Me 410 is hit and burns — a symbol of the end.

Like their comrades of the fighter planes, the *Zerstörer* units were not able to keep the terror of bomb attacks away from the German cities. This picture shows the center of Koblenz in the spring of 1945.

Afterword

Bf 110's were never as successful as their American counterpart, the P 38 "Lightning." This was not the fault of the men who flew their Bf 110's against the enemy with great courage and sacrifice. As in so many great technical errors in planning, the guilt belonged to the bureaucrats and technocrats of the Reich Air Ministry, as well as the leadership of the Luftwaffe at that time. In these circles — for whatever reasons — they were not ready to recognize the quickly advancing technical development of military aviation. This neglect was paid for by thousands with their lives, and not just *Zerstörer* pilots — to say nothing of the effects on the civilian population.

Much has already been said and written about the insanity of war in general and World War II in particular. May all of this be a lesson and a warning to future generations. The political world of today, though, gives little reason for hope. All the same, we would like to close the book with this thought:

"To honor the dead and warn the living"

Schiffer Military History
Specializing in the German Military of World War II

Panzerkorps *Grossdeutschland* Helmuth Spaeter. The elite *GD* Panzerkorps and its divisions, *GD, Brandenburg, Führer Begleit,* and *Kurmark* are covered in this volume, including their formation and battle histories during World War II. An extensive listing of *Knight's Cross* winners rounds out this comprehensive pictorial.
Size: 7 3/4" x 10 1/2" 248 pp.
Over 500 photos, maps, documents, charts
ISBN: 0-88740-245-3　　　　hard cover　　　　　　　　　　$24.95

Stuka Pilot Hans-Ulrich Rudel Günther Just. Hans-Ulrich Rudel was the only soldier in World War II to receive the highest German decoration for bravery–the *Golden Oak Leaves with Swords and Diamonds to the Knight's Cross*. This book by one of his fellow officers covers his entire life's story in many never before published photographs and reminiscences by family members, friends, and those who flew with him.
Size: 8 1/2" x 11"   Over 400 photos 280 pp.
ISBN: 0-88740-252-6　　　　hard cover　　　　　　　　　　$29.95

The *HG* Panzer Division Alfred Otte. This panzer division was formed from the Luftwaffe and took the name of its commander-in-chief, Herman Göring. It was originally formed as a motorized police unit, however, it later became a panzer regiment and eventually expanded to divisional size. The *HG* Panzer Division fought in the African Campaign, the Italian Campaign, on the eastern and western fronts and in the final defense of Germany. This is their story.
Size: 7 3/4" x 10 1/2" 176 pp.
325 b/w photographs, maps, documents
ISBN: 0-88740-206-2　　　　hard cover　　　　　　　　　　$24.95

German Military Rifles and Machine Pistols 1871-1945 Hans Dieter Götz. This richly illustrated volume portrays the development of the modern German weapons and their ammunition, and includes many rare and experimental types. Among the weapons covered in this book are the Werder rifle, Mauser rifles, the various M/71 rifles and ammunition, the 88 cartridge, the Infantry Rifle 88, the 98 rifles, the Fallschirmjäger rifle, the 41 & 43 rifles, ERMA & Walther machine pistols and many more. Value guide included.
Size: 8 1/2" x 11"   248pp.
Many documents, drawings, and over 200 photos
ISBN: 0-88740-264-X　　　　hard cover　　　　　　　　　　$35.00

The Waffen-SS Herbert Walther. This interesting pictorial and factual documentation presents the history of the Waffen-SS from their initial formation to the end of the war. Over 500 photographs, many taken in the heat of battle, show the Waffen-SS divisions on many fronts, in victory and in defeat. This book explains in words and pictures the development of the Waffen-SS and their place in modern history.
Size: 7 3/4" x 10 1/2" 240 pp.
500+ b/w photographs
ISBN: 0-88740-204-6　　　　hard cover　　　　　　　　　　$24.95